MODERN GUITAR RIGS

Second Edition

music **PRO** guides

MODERN GUITAR RIGS

THE TONE FANATIC'S GUIDE TO INTEGRATING AMPS AND EFFECTS

Second Edition

SCOTT KAHN

Hal Leonard Books
An Imprint of Hal Leonard Corporation

Second edition published in 2014
by Hal Leonard Books
An Imprint of Hal Leonard Corporation
7777 West Bluemound Road
Milwaukee, WI 53213

Trade Book Division Editorial Offices
33 Plymouth Street, Montclair, NJ 07042

First edition published in 2011
by Hal Leonard Books

Book design by Adam Fulrath

Artwork and Illustration Credits:
Illustrations 2.1, 2.2, 2.3, 4.1, 5.1 by Bronwen Weger
Illustrations 6.1, 6.2, 10.16b by Scott Kahn
Illustration 3.16b by Scott Kahn and Bronwen Weger
Rig photos (John Petrucci, Steven Wilson, John Wesley, Steve Stevens) by Scott Kahn, courtesy of MusicPlayers.com
Photos 3.2, 3.3, 3.6, 4.9, 6.4, 6.9, 9.15, 10.16 and 10.16a by Scott Kahn, courtesy of MusicPlayers.com
Screen shots 1.1, 3.17, 6.9c by Scott Kahn
Rig diagrams and rig photos (Alex Lifeson) by Scott Appleton
Illustrations 8.1, 10.4 courtesy of RJM Music Technology
Illustration 10.1 courtesy of Radial Engineering
Illustration 10.2 courtesy of Guitar Laboratory
Illustration 10.3 courtesy of Voodoo Lab
Photos 10.11b, 10.11c, 10.11d by Matthew Schieferstein
Unless otherwise specified above, all product photos and illustrations provided courtesy of their respective manufacturers.

Printed in the United States of America

The Library of Congress has cataloged the first edition as follows:

Kahn, Scott.
  Modern guitar rigs : the tone fanatic's guide to integrating amps & effects / Scott Kahn.
    p. cm.
  Includes bibliographical references.
1. Electric guitar. 2. Guitar--Electronic equipment. I. Title.
ML1015.G9K34 2011
787.87'192--dc23

ISBN 978-1-4803-5515-6

www.halleonardbooks.com

Contents

Contents

Acknowledgments

Special thanks to the Members of the Academy . . . er, my "technical oversight committee." These are some of the great amp and effects builders I called upon during the course of writing this book to make sure that guys with bigger rigs than mine won't tear me apart in the forums for saying things they disagree with:

Ron Menelli, RJM Music Technology
Kyle Rhodes, Rhodes Amplification

Thanks to the following superstars, their techs, and their rig designers, who gave me unprecedented access to the innermost workings of their rigs:

John Petrucci
Alex Lifeson
Steven Wilson
John Wesley
Matthew "Maddi" Schieferstein
Scott Appleton
Mark Snyder

Thanks to the following rig builders who provided some candid insight into their rig-building design philosophies and the tools they use:

Bob Bradshaw
David Phillips and Martin Golub
David Friedman

Good thing we're not at the Grammys. They would have kicked me off the stage by now! My thanks continue:

To John Quigley, senior editor at MusicPlayers.com, who made sure this text didn't put players like him to sleep. And to Derek Davodowich, senior editor and bandmate, for letting me tear apart his rigs to test these products.

A very special thanks to my colleagues at all of the great companies making gear for pro guitar rigs! There are too many of you to list by name, but you know who you are, and you know what a pest I was over the past few months, too!

And finally, thank you to the readers of MusicPlayers.com and to all of my online friends at Huge Racks Inc., The Gear Page, and Rig-Talk. Your constant discussion and questions about these topics inspired me to write this book.

Megan and Dylan, you're supposed to be asleep now!

CHAPTER 1

Modern Guitar Rigs Defined

A guitar, an instrument cable, and a combo amp walked into a bar seeking great tone and flexibility. At the end of the bar sat a real knockout. She had a couple of half stacks, pedals to suit her every whim, and one look at her rig told you that she could go from smooth and cool to fiery hot with just the touch of her toe to a footswitch.

If your idea of the ultimate guitar rig is a single-channel combo amp and an overdrive pedal, this is definitely *not* the book for you. But if you crave the flexibility of multiple amps, wet/dry rigs, numerous effects without the tap-dance routine, multiple speaker cabinets, reliability in a concert venue setting, and wireless freedom—the short list—then you've come to the right place.

I don't mean to imply that a combo amp can't be part of a pro rig. Anyone playing a nice Two-Rock or Fuchs (or other boutique) combo is unlikely to fall into the "amateur" category, but those gear setups don't really qualify as *rigs* in my book (interpret that however you like).

A *guitar rig* by my definition is the complete collection of tools used in delivering your sound. The rig includes your amp(s), speaker cabinets, effects pedals, and rack gear such as effects, tuners, loopers, wireless system, power conditioners, foot controllers and pedalboards, and all the other little stuff that ties it all together. Your guitars may be included in the description of your rig as well, since some guitars add very specific capabilities that would otherwise be missing from the rig (piezo acoustic output, MIDI pickups for guitar synths, etc.). A nice combo amp might be one component *in* your rig, but if that's all you've got, you have an amp, not a rig.

My love affair with guitar began back in 1985 with a solid-state Peavey Bandit 65 combo amp. (Cut me some slack. I was only a teenager.) The built-in distortion was selectable via footswitch, sounded way better than my friend's RAT distortion pedal, and my tone rivaled all the great shredders of the '80s, at least in my mind.

I very quickly discovered the world of effects pedals, stringing a chorus, phaser, flanger, and delay in front of the amp and playing with a wide range of cool sounds. Effects loops and buffers? Who knew about those? And, none of the BOSS or DOD pedals back then featured *true bypass*.

It wasn't easy to change more than a couple of effects at once, either, or switch from a clean sound to distortion while also changing an effect. How many times did I miss nailing the first beat of the chorus back then? We dare not answer that question in print.

You can pretty much guess where things went from there in my quest for instant control over my increasingly complex rig: multi-effects processors, rack gear, MIDI foot controllers, audio loops, wet-dry rigs, and tube amps, of course. Oh, and my guitar playing improved a bit, too!

In the '80s and '90s, building a professional guitar rig was not an easy task. Rack-based effects processors, many just "borrowed" from the recording studio environment, were complex to program—and usually operated at different signal levels from guitar amps. MIDI foot controllers, while simple to operate, were especially complex when it came to programming. You almost had to understand the basics of computer programming if you had any hope of configuring this gear for yourself. And without Internet forums in which to post questions, help was much harder to obtain. It was during this era that custom rack builders like Bob Bradshaw of Custom Audio Electronics were busy beyond belief building guitar rigs for the stars.

Fig. 1.1: This editing software from Psicraft Designs lets users of the TC Electronic G-System configure complex system levels and MIDI functions with ease, right from the computer while you're playing.

Today, Bob is still building rigs to die for, but advances in technology have had a significant impact on the tools available to the modern guitar player. New gear is much easier to program and no longer requires a degree in rocket science to comprehend, thanks primarily to the popular use of computer-based editors. Rather than trying to decipher a one- or two-line, twenty-character display on a rackmounted multi-effects processor, computer-based editors give you an entire computer screen from which to select your options, tweak your sounds, and customize how you interact with your gear.

Today, you can build a complex rig for yourself without requiring assistance from the big guys, and at a price point that is far lower than it used to be. Of course, if you've only done your gear shopping at the big chain stores, you haven't been exposed to the majority of products that exist for building your dream rig. Boutique builders have created a huge range of products to solve virtually every challenge you may face in designing your dream rig, but it's rare that you find their products sitting on the shelf at the local music megastore.

You don't need to be touring the world to have a pro guitar rig. In fact, even if you're just an indie rocker playing at the local club level, a pro rig can make a huge difference. Ever play shows with multiple bands where you're given ten or fifteen minutes to set up everything? How many times have you stressed out over getting your half stack set up, your pedalboard in place, connecting all the power cables, running audio cables to and from your amp and effects loop, and then running out of time trying to tune up your guitar and also troubleshoot the ground loop you didn't hear at last night's show?

Now imagine this scenario: popping the doors off the front and back of a rack that houses your entire rig—even amp heads, then connecting a speaker cable, power cable, and one cable run to your foot controller. A pro guitar rig at the club level means you may actually have time to enjoy a drink with your singer (and the groupies) before the show while your drummer and keyboard player are still setting up.

In this book, we'll look at the technologies and products available for building pro guitar rigs, talk with custom rig builders, and explore actual rigs played by some of our favorite guitarists. As you'll discover, MIDI isn't some big, scary thing you need to be frightened of, and building complex rigs can greatly simplify your setup, leaving you more time to focus on playing. In fact, you'll soon discover that what initially seems like a complex rig is actually quite simple to understand and implement for yourself.

Throughout these chapters, I highlight specific pieces of gear from various manufacturers that are widely used by professional musicians in building their guitar rigs. But many of the companies I mention in this book offer an even wider range of gear to solve your pro rig design issues. If a product I talk about sounds like it *almost* meets your needs, be sure to visit that manufacturer's website to explore their full range of products (contact info can be found at the end of the book). Many of these products have been reviewed in-depth at MusicPlayers.com, the online magazine for serious musicians, so look there for more extensive details regarding some of the items discussed in this book.

There are other companies building products that serve the pro rig market, too. With small one-person shops cropping up regularly, it's hard to stay on top of all of them, and if I neglected to mention your favorite accessory company, consider it an oversight and not a lack of endorsement for their products. The companies whose products *are* mentioned in this book, though, are builders who make products that serious musicians routinely choose to implement in their rigs.

CHAPTER 2

Effects Loops

I f you like to use effects, especially the kind that fall into the time-based categories—delay, modulation, reverb, etc., it's almost essential for your amp to have an *effects loop* for optimal tone. But don't worry if your vintage amp lacks an effects loop—as you'll read below, it's simple enough to add a loop to your amp without modifying the equipment.

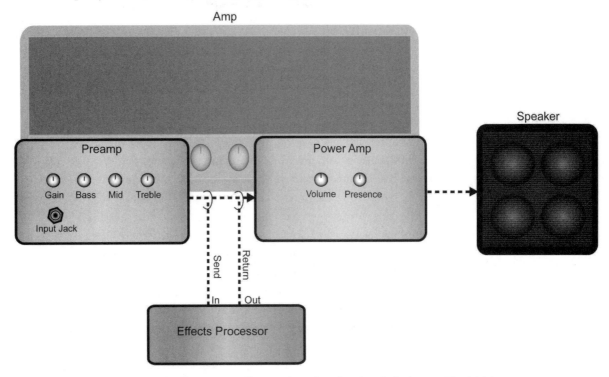

With an effects loop, your effects typically get placed in the signal chain in between the preamp and power amp section of your amp. There are entire books dedicated to effects and their placement. In this book, we'll assume you know where you want to put your effects in the signal chain for optimal tone, and we'll just focus on making your rig sound its best.

Fig. 2.1: It's easy to connect effects to your rig using the amplifier's effects loop.

There are two different approaches to implementing effects loops—*series* and *parallel*, and they each have their pros and cons.

Series Loops

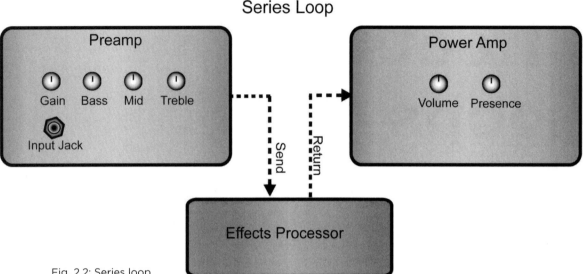

Series Loop

Fig. 2.2: Series loop

With a series (or serial) effects loop, 100 percent of the sound from the preamp section of your amp passes through the *Effects Send* output to your external gear, and then the processed sound comes back into the amp through the *Effects Return*, or *Returns* if the amp features a stereo loop.

Although this can sound fantastic with your time-based effects, in the case of modern multi-effects processors, your entire audio signal passes through an analog-to-digital conversion and then (after processing) a digital-to-analog conversion before being returned to the effects loop. While this conversion may not be audibly discernable in many high-end effects units, there are some tone purists who insist that it compromises their tone.

If you have rack gear more than a few years old, though, this will definitely be a problem for the series loop and your tone. A digital effects processor from the '80s may have only 8-bit or 12-bit A/D converters, while modern gear today has 24-bit converters. Since your signal is essentially getting sampled—converted to a digital format—the older, lower-resolution converters definitely degrade the signal quality, which will compromise your tone unless you can pass some dry signal directly through your amp without running it into the effects loop.

Obviously if you just have analog pedals in your effects loop, there will be no A/D/A conversion taking place at all, but the pedals may color your tone in some way even when the pedals aren't engaged.

Parallel Loops

In a parallel effects loop, a small mixer circuit inside the amp splits the signal from the preamp section and sends part of it directly to the power amp section and part of it to the effects loop. A mix control on the amp enables you to control how much signal is sent to the effects loop and how much of the signal is passed to the power amp dry (unprocessed). Many modern amps with parallel effects loops have the ability to be set to 100 percent wet, effectively turning them into a series loop.

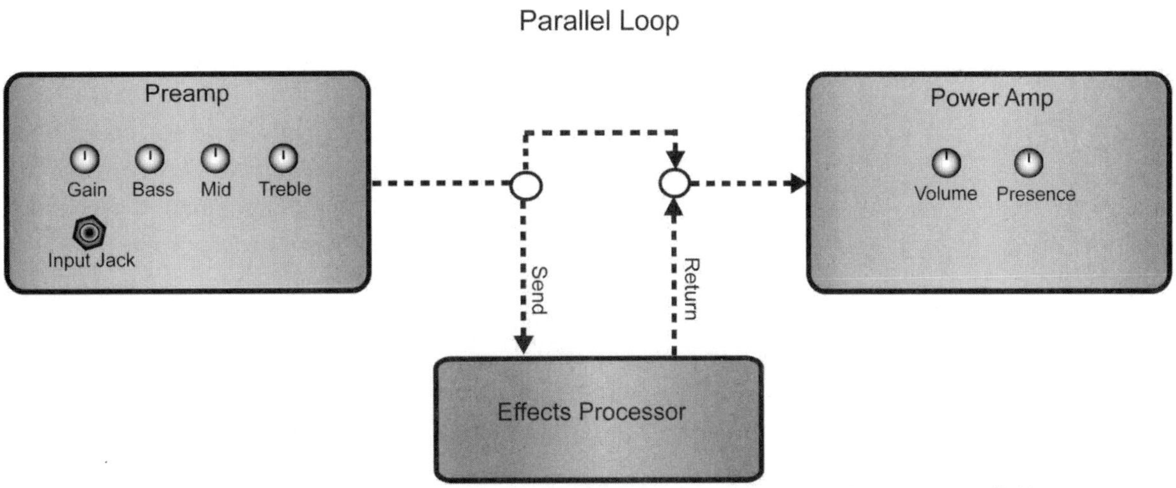

Parallel Loop

Fig. 2.3: Parallel loop

Testing Your Loop: You Might Not Have What You Think You Have

On some older amps, and others that have poorly designed loops, there's no guarantee that your series loop is 100 percent in series, nor is there a guarantee that your parallel loop's 100 percent wet setting is truly in series. You can (and should) test your amp's effects loop to make sure of its behavior.

All it takes is a simple tuner or other pedal to conduct a test of your loop. Take a send from the effects loop to the pedal, and don't connect its output to a loop return. If your loop is wired in series, you shouldn't hear any output from your guitar without connecting the return. In a parallel loop, if you've set the mix ratio to 100 percent wet and you can hear some guitar, then obviously the loop is not really sending 100 percent of the signal into the pedal—it's not a true series loop. This seems obvious, but you'd be surprised just how many amps have loops that don't function exactly as specified.

The Right Loop for the Job

Neither circuit is specifically better or worse than the other, but which one is right for your rig depends in part on the effects you plan to place in the loop. Most modern multi-effects processors have advanced mixers built in, and while your entire guitar signal may pass into one of these devices through a series loop, you get full control over the wet/dry levels for each of the individual effects within the processor that are present in your signal chain.

The trickiest thing you'll deal with is optimizing the level of your sends and returns to/from the loop, and the input/output levels on the effects gear, but you can get gorgeous tone through a series loop, and these tend to be the most common loop types on modern amps. With most modern effects processors, you don't have to worry about any degradation of your tone, as the analog/digital converters are of much higher quality than those found in older rack gear from the '80s and '90s.

Although you can run pedals in your effects loop, the loop is best utilized by rack gear—particularly multi-effects processors or dedicated time-based effects like delay and reverb units. Most effects loops are designed to accommodate the line-level output from rack gear (+4 dBu), and some have level controls (either switches for +4 dBu/–10 dBV operation or actual level controls) to accommodate rack gear or pedals. But some amps (like the classic Soldano SLO-100) have loops fixed to +4 dBu, which means that some vintage effects may need a boost to output an adequate volume level. *Custom Audio Electronics and MXR make a nice Boost/Line Driver pedal that simplifies matching the output of your effect to your loop or other part of your signal chain.*

When using a multi-effects processor in a parallel loop, for best results it is essential that the device offers a *Kill Dry* feature. The Kill Dry feature configures the effects processor to output 100 percent wet (processed) signals. This is important because if you have a dry signal passing straight through your amp from the preamp to the power amp, and part of the signal running through your multi-effects processor is un-effected (but has still passed through an A/D and a D/A conversion) and arrives at the output slightly delayed from the "real" dry signal, these dual unprocessed signal paths may experience a comb filter effect (which can sound like a cocked wah sound or a flanger), resulting in compromised sound quality.

➔ If you're an analog pedal lover, parallel loops may be preferable to series loops since you don't have the advanced mixing capabilities found within digital multi-effects processors. Also, your noisy vintage pedals won't completely destroy your tone, since you will still have some percentage of your unprocessed tone routed directly to the power block section of your amplifier.

➔ If you want to build a wet/dry rig, a parallel loop is *sometimes* preferable, since you can maintain a 100 percent un-effected dry signal running straight through your amp to the dry cabinet while a percentage of your signal gets routed to the wet portion of your rig through the Effects Send. With some series loops, plugging into only the Send for your effects (but not the Return) will kill the dry signal completely. *Many Mesa/Boogie amps work in this fashion. However, these amps frequently have a Slave Output that can be used to send a signal to your effects for a Wet/Dry rig.*

➔ If you rely on a modern digital multi-effects processor, it's easy to mix all of your effects levels within the processor, thus favoring a series loop. It's straightforward and simple to implement, and most pros go for the simple approach.

➔ If your amp has a series loop but you crave the flexibility of a parallel loop, or you just refuse to allow your entire signal to be converted from analog to digital and back, a *line mixer* can be used to split your signal so that 100 percent of it doesn't run through your effects gear, effectively creating a parallel loop for your effects. We'll talk about mixers for guitar rigs in depth later in this book.

Making Your Series Loop Run in Parallel

While line mixers can be used to add parallel capabilities to an amp with a series loop, there are a few compact solutions that can easily split the signal in your series loop to allow some of your dry signal to pass straight through to the effects return.

Suhr MiniMix II

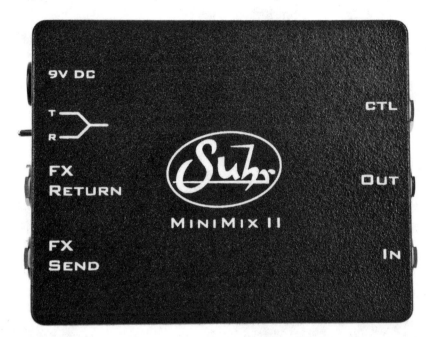

Fig. 2.4: Suhr MiniMix II

Suhr Guitars is mostly known for its incredible guitars, but the company also makes a handful of utility products that some serious heavyweights swear by. One such device is the MiniMix II. If you have one amp, a series loop, and an old-but-great multi-effects processor, just hook this up to make a significant improvement in your tone—just be sure to activate the effects unit's Kill Dry feature or otherwise set it to 100 percent wet output. The MiniMix II can also accept a mono input from a second effects unit.

Carl Martin Paraloop

Almost identical in function to the Suhr MiniMix II, the Paraloop provides another option for adding some parallel goodness to your series loop if desired, but also provides an adjustable mix control.

Fig. 2.5: Carl Martin Paraloop

Xotic Effects X-Blender

Fig. 2.6:
Xotic Effects
X-Blender

The X-Blender is similar to the other loop pedals, but also has series loop capabilities. In this mode, the controls are disabled (other than the active/ bypass button) and the signal is not buffered.

No Effects Loop? No Problem!

Just because your vintage amp lacks an effects loop is no reason to have to miss the party. On one hand, you could send your amp to a builder for a custom retrofit. But if you have a valuable classic amp, modifying it isn't going to be a likely scenario. Fortunately, it's easy enough to add an external effects loop to your amp without resorting to scalpels, provided you're willing to embrace the idea of a wet/dry rig, which will be discussed in detail later in this book.

Suhr ISO Line-Out Box

The ISO box provides a transformer-isolated output from your amp to send to your effects. It taps the speaker output of your amp and provides an audio pass-through that must be connected to your speaker cabinet (it's not a load box).

Once you send the isolated output from the ISO box to your effects processor or loop system, you then take the output from your effects and send the audio signal to a mono or stereo amp and related speakers to build a wet/dry rig.

Fig. 2.7: Suhr ISO Line-Out Box

CHAPTER 3

Rack Gear Overview

Rack gear has long been the serious shredder's path to ultimate flexibility, and with the surging popularity of music influenced by '80s rockers, I've seen renewed interest in guitar rigs that provide extreme flexibility (hence this book, which would have gone over like a lead weight if it were released during the grunge rock years). Why settle for three or four amp channels when you can store a seemingly infinite number of amp tones and crazy effects (from pedals or rack gear), all accessible at the touch of a single button on a foot controller?

Rack gear is rarely in the spotlight these days, but the list of pro players with at least *some* rack gear in their rigs is endless. And by the time you're finished with this book, if you didn't previously own any rack gear, you probably will very soon.

Today there are more new rack products for guitar players than ever before, even if you don't spot many of these at your local music store chain. Back in the '80s, most guitarists were taking signal-processing gear from recording studios and putting it in their guitar rigs with varying degrees of success (and complexity) as they sought effects that had better audio quality than most pedals offered, but these days, almost everything you'd like to put in your rack has been designed expressly with guitar players in mind. Plus, you can easily rack your pedals and have instant control over the whole collection with single-button simplicity.

From tube preamps and power amps to digital modelers, pro tuners, wireless systems, analog pedal loopers, and multi-effects processors, there's a huge assortment of rack gear designed to take your guitar inspiration (and tone) to a higher level.

Rack gear isn't just for players who like a ton of effects. As I mentioned, virtually every touring pro has at least some rack gear in his or her rig—effects or not. Rack gear provides supreme flexibility for any style of guitar player looking to simplify his or her use of multiple amp tones and effects. This might include making use of specialized studio effects, or it might just be a way to simplify the madness of tap-dancing across a pedalboard stocked with your favorite boutique pedals.

This chapter covers products that can either work with your existing amp or replace it entirely, providing a wide range of options including amps, effects processors, power conditioners, wireless systems, and much more.

Most guitar players only use a single amp and a few pedals, so getting started with rack gear can seem like a daunting ordeal. Where do you start if you haven't made the leap yet? You may have been discouraged by crazy stories from friends and things you've read in online forums, such as the complexity of programming rack gear, that tube gear in a rack doesn't sound as good as a head, that you have to learn MIDI, and more.

As you'll discover, there's a lot of misinformation in the public domain, and "rack gear" comprises a broad collection of products that can take your guitar tone to new levels of excellence.

Rack Gear Defined

Simply put, "rack gear" is any piece of music equipment or accessory that is built within a 19-inch-wide chassis that can be screwed into an equipment rack. But even that simple description doesn't tell the whole story.

For players using rack gear to control effects pedals (stomp boxes), those pedals can easily be placed on standard 19-inch-wide shelves (or in drawers) for use alongside more traditional rack gear.

Players who love their amp heads can have those full-size giants loaded into custom-built rack cases that can hold the heads along with standard 19-inch rack gear. Virtually all the pros on major tours have rigs built like this—even their 4x12 speaker cabinets travel in custom cases and racks, but the weekend club player can also benefit from a similar kind of setup.

Some of the advantages of rack gear can be experienced immediately by anyone playing live shows on a regular basis, whether it's a pro tour or you're just hitting the local bars and clubs on weekends. Your pricey gear can be extremely well protected inside of equipment racks, many of which are rated to meet airline transportation or military specs, and if your entire rig is contained within a single rack, setup time at a gig can take less than one minute—just plug in three or four cables and you're all set!

Rack gear tends to fall into three primary categories of products:

→Amps: guitar preamps and power amps specifically designed for installation into 19-inch racks.

→Effects: multi-effects processors or dedicated effect processors (like delay or reverb units, or even rackmounted wah systems).

→Accessories: pedal loopers (for controlling your stomp boxes), tuners, wireless receivers, power conditioners, and more.

Rack Guitar Amplifiers

Guitar players have been sticking their heads in racks for decades (heck, we've put our heads up our . . . well, you know). In fact, one of the first options came from Mesa/Boogie, whose classic Mark II and IV heads were available in 19-inch-wide enclosures that could be rackmounted without any custom modifications.

But when we discuss rack amps today, we're typically referring to modular gear. Rackmounted guitar amps provide the ultimate flexibility when it comes to tone. The preamps and power amps, which collectively make up your traditional head or combo amp, are each contained in a separate, rackmountable chassis.

The advantage of this design is that it provides very flexible tone options—more than you'll find with virtually any traditional tube amp or head. You can mix a preamp from one company with a power amp from another to create a truly one-of-a-kind signature tone, or select from among multiple power amp options within a single company to get just the kind of tone you desire.

For example, Mesa/Boogie has multiple power amps with 6L6 power tubes, as well as one with EL-84 tubes. Within the 6L6 tube family, Mesa/Boogie's power amps offer vastly different power ratings as well as other differences in design (Simul-class, dual rectifier, etc.) that each contribute to a significantly different guitar tone.

It's not just about 6L6 vs. EL-34 power amps, either. Many rackable tube preamps contain memory for storing multiple presets. Rather than just choosing between a couple of channels, like with a typical two- or three-channel head, imagine a head that lets you dial in your amp tone and then save a hundred different presets! Using any popular MIDI foot controller, you can have direct access to multiple different sounds within a single preamp.

Just because there may be digital technology at work for selecting your sounds, there's no need to worry about your tone. The sound from racked preamp and power amps can still be 100 percent tube, and the most popular preamps all feature multiple 12AX7 or ECC83 tubes just like your favorite traditional amp. Likewise, power amps feature the usual assortment of power amp tubes (6L6, EL-34, EL-84, etc.). And usually, these preamps and power amps have simple, familiar knobs with which to dial in your tone.

Not all guitar preamps feature tubes, however. There are numerous solid-state guitar preamps on the market, not to mention a wide variety of modeling products that can all be paired with tube power amps to combine tonal variety with tube warmth.

Another great advantage of rackable preamps: stereo operation! Almost all rackable guitar preamps offer stereo effects returns and stereo master outputs, a great option for players who love crazy spatial effects and delays.

Popular Rackable Preamps

For extreme flexibility and tube goodness, you can't beat preamps such as the ENGL e580, Mesa/Boogie Triaxis, Egnater M4 and Randall RM4, or even the recently discontinued Marshall JMP-1. Analog purists who don't need the whole kitchen sink but want at least a few traditional amp channels can find bliss in the ENGL e530 Modern or Mesa/Boogie Rectifier Recording Preamp, which have simple two- and three-channel interfaces nearly identical to what you'd find on a head or combo.

Figs. 3.1 and 3.2: Rack preamps from Mesa/Boogie and ENGL are all tube, and just as easy to use as traditional amps.

If you're a modeling fan, it's hard to beat the flexibility of modeling amps and profilers like the Fractal Audio Axe-FX Ultra, Line 6 POD HD Pro, or Kemper Profiling Amplifier. Besides modeling classic tube amps, these products also include built-in multi-effects processors for added flexibility (not to mention a host of other special features).

For players seeking a non-modeled, solid-state (analog) preamp tone, options abound for you, too. Check out the Rocktron Prophesy II or Voodoo Lab Guitar Preamp to hear what you can do without tubes or modeling in the preamp section.

Fig. 3.3: The Rocktron Prophesy 2 is a non-tube preamp with onboard effects.

The used gear market is another source of popular rackable preamps. The Marshall JMP-1 MIDI Tube Preamp was only recently discontinued, but enjoys a huge following from pro players and amateurs alike, and we know more than a few players who still love the classic ADA MP-1, not to mention a variety of preamps that were made by Peavey almost twenty years ago.

In almost all cases, dialing in your sound on a rack preamp involves the same process as with your traditional heads and combos. You turn knobs for gain and EQ, loop levels, etc., hit a few buttons or flip a few switches for different preamp voicing options, and then maybe push a few buttons to save your settings in the preamp's memory.

In the case of simple two-channel preamps like the Mesa/Boogie Rectifier Recording Preamp, you just dial in your settings and play. The very intimidating-looking Triaxis has soft membrane buttons for changing your "virtual" knob values, but don't be scared: inside it's all analog.

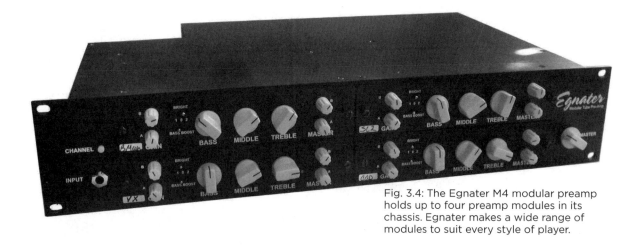

Fig. 3.4: The Egnater M4 modular preamp holds up to four preamp modules in its chassis. Egnater makes a wide range of modules to suit every style of player.

Fig. 3.5: The Mesa/Boogie Triaxis tube preamp is filled with classic Mark Series tone.

Popular Rackable Power Amps

It should come as no surprise that many of the companies building tube preamps also offer a variety of power amps. Check out the wide range of all-tube stereo power amps from ENGL, Mesa/Boogie, Randall, Marshall, Carvin, and Fryette.

If you're looking to test the waters first, the used market has plenty of old Peavey and Marshall rackable tube power amps. I still have a Peavey Classic 50/50 (not to be confused with a similar-named combo amp) loaded with EL-84 tubes in my studio.

Fig. 3.6: Popular power amps from Fryette, Mesa/Boogie, and ENGL.

Rackmounted Amps, Too!

Mesa/Boogie made rack-ready versions of some classic amps including the fantastic Mark IV, and I've even seen Bad Cat build one of their heads into a custom 19-inch enclosure. If you're interested in something modern and very special, check out boutique amp builder Rhodes Amplification. Kyle Rhodes is building new, rack-optimized multi-channel tube amplifiers in single enclosures: separate power amps not needed!

Fig. 3.7: The Rhodes Assassin is a complete amplifier built into a standard 19-inch rack chassis for easy integration into a pro rig.

Rack Effects Processors

One of the most popular categories of rack gear for guitar players is *multi-effects processors.* It's very easy to replace a large number of pedals from your pedalboard—such as modulation, delay, reverb, compressor, and tuner pedals—with a single device that includes all of these effects and more (pitch shifting, noise gates, filters, wahs, etc.).

Before multi-effects processors came along, guitar players would ransack studio gear to build guitar rigs capable of replicating their album tones and effects. One of the most popular digital delay processors of all time is the TC Electronic 2290, which is still a highly sought-after processor on the used market. You can obtain similar delay sounds from newer TC Electronic gear (and delay units from other companies), but none of those products are built with the same functionality (or analog circuitry) as this legendary product.

Fig. 3.8: The TC Electronic 2290 delay is widely used despite its age and limited availability on the used market thanks to its great sound.

Eventide's line of studio harmonizers was widely implemented in guitar rigs, and eventually Eventide released a few models optimized for use in guitar rigs. Today some players still use studio-grade Eventide gear, but the company's guitarist-friendly Eclipse makes more sense for all but the truly obsessed (and budget-ignorant). Eventide's line of pedals offers the best option, though. They deliver exceptional sounding effects in much easier to operate packages and still have advanced editing and MIDI capabilities if you need it.

Also popular in the early days of rack systems were rack processors from Korg, Yamaha, and Roland. You'll routinely find players touting the merits of these products in online forums.

Multi-effects processors are a great place to start exploring the world of rack gear. These products can open you up to a whole new world of fantastic sounds, and since the footswitches aren't built in (as with your pedals), you control these processors via MIDI foot controllers. If your needs are very effect specific, then skip the complexity of a multi-effects unit and get a dedicated delay or reverb unit.

With MIDI foot controllers, you can instantly select from multiple presets that you've saved, and you can also turn individual effect blocks on and off, just as if you were stepping on individual pedals on a pedalboard. For example, one preset may have your chorus, delay, and reverb enabled, while another preset may have a compressor and reverb. But once you've selected a preset, you can go further and step on the switches on your foot controller to turn individual effects on or off within the preset.

One distinguishing feature among various multi-effects processors has to do with whether the product has a preamp circuit built in. Obviously, all of the modeling products do, but some multi-effects processors such as the classic (old) Lexicon MPX-G2 also have preamps or drive/distortion circuits. Most multi-effects processors do *not* have preamp circuits, though, and I think this is a smart design omission. There's too much circuitry needed for good preamps to fit in the box with an effects unit. Start with great tone from your tube amp or preamp, or run a favorite stomp box in front of the amp, and then used these rack products for effects other than distortion and overdrive.

Popular Multi-Effects Processors

Today, processors like the TC Electronic G-Major 2 (and the G-Major before it) are among the most popular products for guitar players looking to add some rackable effects to their rigs, thanks to their studio-quality sound, easy programmability, guitarist-optimized features, and very reasonable pricing. For the cost of a pair of premium pedals, you can put a lot of creative power in your rig and eliminate the use of many pedals. Players looking for an easy path into rack-based effects processing should check out the G-Major 2 and G-Major, along with the DigiTech GSP1101 and Rocktron Xpression.

If you've set your sights higher and you've got a bigger budget, popular effects processors used by touring and recording pros *also* include the Eventide Eclipse, TC Electronic G-Force, Fractal Audio Axe-FX, and the TC Electronic G-System.

Fig. 3.9: The TC Electronic G-Major 2 provides great sound and simple programmability.

Figs. 3.10–3.12: The best modern effects processors today include the Eclipse, G-System, and Axe-FX.

Of course the true cost for most of these products increases once you add a foot controller (except for the G-System, which includes a foot controller) plus the actual rack case to hold your gear, so don't forget to factor in theses additional costs when considering implementing rack gear in your rig.

For studio use and home recording, you can control effects processors from their front panels without needing a foot controller—you just won't have instant on/off access to effect blocks unless you're able to hit the tiny buttons on the display panels with your toes while you're playing.

On the used market, some classic multi-effects processors that are still widely respected include the previously mentioned Lexicon MPX-G2 and a variety of processors from ART, BOSS, and Korg. However, considering how much technology has improved, if you're excited about adding some rack effects to your rig, I'd strongly recommend investing in new gear. You'll have a much easier time editing effects (many new products have computer-based software editors), and while the audio quality of some vintage rack effects is great, those devices don't always provide instantaneous transitions from one sound preset to another. You don't want an audible click or gap each time you step on a button to select a new preset.

Most important to consider, though, is that older effects processors have older analog/digital converters. The 8-bit and 12-bit converters in the old gear will degrade your tone if you place one of these units in a series effects loop! If you love vintage/used rack gear, you'll want to use it in a parallel loop or run it through a line mixer to preserve your tone. New gear like the G-System and G-Major 2 feature the latest 24-bit converters and don't mess with your tone (assuming you've got proper cabling and good signal levels set up).

Popular Single-Effect Processors

For processors with singular functions, there are numerous dedicated reverb units from Lexicon, Eventide, and TC Electronic, and the TC Electronic D-Two digital delay has some very cool capabilities that aren't even available in other products, such as the ability to manually tap in rhythmic patterns for your repeats.

Also hard to come by on the used market, but highly desired, is a series of rackmounted effects processors from Line 6: the Mod Pro, Echo Pro, and Filter Pro. These boxes took Line 6's modeling-pedal technology and added extensive MIDI control, tap tempo and MIDI clock sync, and memory for tons of presets. If you want the sound of those rare rack effects today, be sure to check out the Line 6 POD HD Pro, which contains virtually all of the effects from the individual effects processors, plus a whole range of other capabilities, including amp modeling and computer-based effects editing.

Fig. 3.13: The TC Electronic D-Two digital delay lets you tap in custom delay patterns.

Many pros use the Dunlop Crybaby Wah rackmounted system. The advantage of this is that a long cable run to your foot pedal doesn't carry any audio signals—the actual wah tones are located close to your amp or preamp in the rack, and you just have a wah controller pedal on the floor sending voltage control information back to the rack.

Rackable chorus units are also available. One popular classic is the TC Electronic TC 1210 Spatial Expander + Stereo Chorus/Flanger, still used by numerous pros.

Fig. 3.14: Classic effects processors from Line 6

Fig. 3.15: Dunlop Crybaby Wah—great wah tone without long cable runs.

Eventide's studio-class harmonizers provide an array of effects, including harmonizing, reverb, delay, and modulation, and there was even a guitar-centric GTR 4000 model, but you can get many of these effects from the Eclipse or Eventide's line of Factor effects pedals.

Fig. 3.16: The TC Electronic TC 1210 is one of the best-sounding chorus effects of all time.

What About Floor-Based Multi-Effects?

Products like the BOSS GT-100, Line 6 POD HD 500X, and DigiTech RP1000 have many of the capabilities of rack-based processors, with the added benefit of a built-in foot controller. However, these products rarely provide the same flexibility and premium sound quality as dedicated rack gear, and they almost never have the same level of MIDI capability as dedicated foot controllers. Some of these products are quite capable, though, and do have pro-level audio specs.

We know a lot of touring guitarists who have implemented the TC Electronic Nova System, incorporating it into their pedalboards and replacing numerous other pedals with it (or replacing their big pedalboards entirely with the Nova System for fly-away gigs). Products like this one raise the bar for floor-based products, as they deliver studio-quality tone in a compact package.

For players looking at an in-between solution, the Line 6 M9 and M13 also straddle the fine line between the needs of the pro player and the desire to keep things as simple as possible in a self-contained floor unit.

The Signal Chain: The Pros and Cons of Multi-Effects Processors

The placement of effects in your signal chain is a question sure to be on the minds of many players making the leap to rack gear from a pedalboard full of fantastic sounds. Although there are no hard and fast rules when it comes to guitar rigs, there are some popular gear configurations that most players use.

The greatest advantage that pedals (stomp boxes) have over multi-effects processors is the total flexibility you have in setting the order of the signal chain. You can very easily place certain pedals in front of your amp and others in the effects loop.

Filters and wahs, overdrive, and distortion typically get placed in between the guitar and the amp's input jack. Effects like modulation, delay, and reverb typically get placed in an amp's effects loop (post-EQ), while some effects are widely used in either location, depending on your needs.

For example, a noise gate in front of the amp is great for reducing noise from single-coil pickups, whereas a noise gate in the effects loop is great for reducing noise from high-gain preamp sounds. And a chorus pedal can have a great, but different, sound whether it's placed in front of your amp or in the loop—it's really just a personal artistic preference sometimes.

The Four-Cable Method

One challenge with rack effects gear is that you typically have an all-or-nothing approach to effects placement. You may be able to rearrange the sequence of effects, either in front of or behind each other—e.g., place the delay before the chorus, or in parallel (the dry signal gets split to the modulation effect and delay effects, then the results are mixed at the output)—but commonly the entire effects unit has to be run in your amp's effects loop or in front of the input jack (and most rack gear is optimized for loop-only operation with balanced or line-level I/O).

Many popular modeling preamps and effects processors provide multiple inputs and outputs to accommodate your complex signal routing needs, including the TC Electronic G-System (but not G-Major 2), Fractal Audio Axe-FX, DigiTech GSP1101, Line 6 POD HD Pro, and more. The products typically refer to this feature as insert loops that enable you to route some effects to the front of your amp and other effects to your effects loop in order to eliminate the all-or-nothing limitation of many processors. The wiring scheme for making use of the insert loops is commonly called the four-cable method, as this describes how many cables are needed for the connections. When running a stereo rig, a fifth cable is used, sending a pair of outputs to a stereo power amp instead of the typical mono output returning to your amp's effects loop Return.

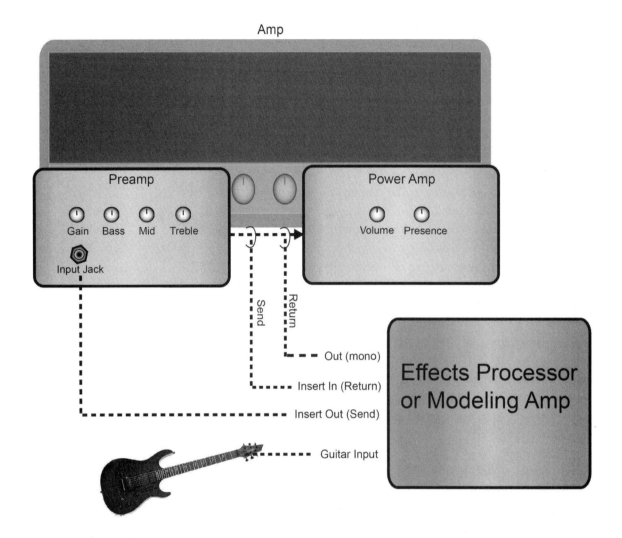

Amp

Preamp

Gain   Bass   Mid   Treble

Input Jack

Power Amp

Volume   Presence

Send

Return

Out (mono)

Insert In (Return)

Insert Out (Send)

Guitar Input

Effects Processor
or Modeling Amp

Fig. 3.17: The four-cable
method enables you to
route some effects from
a modeling amp or multi-
effects processor in front
of your amp and other
effects in the effects loop,
provided that your gear
contains this feature.

Rack Accessories: Foot Controllers, Power Conditioners, Pedal Loopers, Rack Cases, and More

Other chapters in this book will explore in detail the various non-tone-generating components that are found in pro guitar rigs: MIDI foot controllers, power regulators, audio loopers, wireless systems, mixers, custom rack cases, and more.

Programming Rack Gear

Historically, configuring a rack system was quite complex, and many pros turned to professional rig builders to design and configure their rigs. Fortunately, though, electronic musical equipment has gotten much easier to program and configure. If you are comfortable dialing in nice digital delays or selecting voicings for a harmonizer, you've got more than enough skills to program most of the current products. And by *program*, no, we don't mean sitting down at a computer writing lines of Java code. We're talking about setting values for your effects just as if you were twisting knobs on a stomp box, then saving those settings, and finally configuring your MIDI foot controller or other gear to remotely control the product.

Using a product like RJM Music Technology's Effect Gizmo to gain single-button control over a floor (or rack shelf) full of pedals requires zero programming effort—you just push a variety of On/Off buttons for each effect loop and hold down a Write button to save your settings. It really is *that* easy.

Programming your effects has gotten much simpler, too. Historically, we have to attribute the programming horror stories and Internet folklore to gear from Lexicon and Eventide. They built studio gear that required a lot of technical knowledge to program: great for studio engineers, but not so great for guitar players. And even when Lexicon made its guitar-specific MPX-G2, it was still just as complex to program and control via MIDI as any other piece of studio gear—the company just added a few features that made the unit guitar-centric in its effects capabilities.

Happily, the interface on most guitar-related rack effects today is very straightforward. But if you're still feeling technologically challenged, processors like the Fractal Audio Axe-FX, TC Electronic G-Major 2 and G-System, Line 6 POD HD Pro, and BOSS GT-Pro all have computer-based software editors for Macintosh and Windows. Rather than trying to set values on a small two- or three-line display, having an entire computer screen to see everything graphically makes creating the sounds of your dreams quite easy.

Fig. 3.18: With an editor like this one for the G-System, dialing in your effects is easy, and you don't even have to sit on the floor!

Also, the software editors make it very easy to share presets with other musicians. Why reinvent the wheel when you can access a manufacturer's online library of sounds and effects and just add new stuff created by fellow musicians and then just tweak the sounds to taste?

Where to Begin

As you can see, there is a wide range of products that fall under the category of rack gear, and I haven't even discussed the non-musical stuff yet! For the modern guitar player, there are an incredible number of options that can either enhance your current guitar rig or replace it entirely.

If you love your amp, a multi-effects processor is most likely the first item you'll want to start this rack love affair with. Something like the TC Electronic G-Major 2 or Rocktron Xpression can provide a fantastic sonic upgrade to your effects over an assorted pedal collection, and a MIDI foot controller with pedal looper will help you eliminate the pedal tap dance.

If you're looking for some new tones, you can't beat some of the rack preamps and power amps from ENGL and Mesa/Boogie. A Triaxis rig puts the entire collection of Mark series tones in a small package with instant access, while the ENGL rigs can give metal and prog players an extremely diverse range of tones from studio clean to monstrously heavy. The Randall gear lets you mix and match a variety of different preamp modules to build a truly one-of-a-kind amplifier that covers everything from blues and classic rock to modern metal.

If you crave flexibility, options, and stellar tone, break away from the pedal pack. Soon enough, you'll be playing guitar according to my personal mantra: once you go rack, you never go back!

CHAPTER 4

Switching Between Multiple Amps

Two amps. One footswitch. Three or more amps? No problem. There are many reasons why it makes sense to have multiple amps in your guitar rig. The first and simplest reason is that you want the variety of tones that multiple amps can provide.

Wouldn't it be great to get your beautiful "Fender Clean" tone from an actual Fender amp, and then step on a footswitch when you need to cut instantly to your Mesa/Boogie Dual Rectifier for some heavy-metal thunder? Perhaps then switch to your Vox AC-30 for those alt-rock tones?

The second reason for running multiple amps is to run a wet/dry rig. In this case, your dry guitar tone comes out of one amp and your effected (processed) sound comes out of a second amp. Wet/dry rigs are explored in detail in Chapter 5.

Perhaps your amp is filled with lots of great sounds, but only has two or three channels. Pros like Dream Theater's John Petrucci have multiple identical amps in their rigs so that they can have instant access to multiple tones from the same amp.

Finally, imagine you're going on a tour. What would you do if your amp failed in mid performance? If failure to perform isn't an option, then you need a backup. (If only this advice worked for other, ahem, *scenarios*.) After all, you do play more than one guitar, right?

Fortunately, switching from one amp to another at the touch of a footswitch is one of the simplest things you can do with your rig.

Two-Amp Switching

There are numerous pedal-based solutions available, commonly called A/B switches or A/B/Y switches. Operation is pretty straightforward: typically one button lets you switch directly between Amp A and Amp B, while a secondary switch lets you send your signal to both amps at the same time—the "Y" configuration. Running your guitar through a clean amp concurrently with an overdriven amp can yield some incredible new textures (as any player with a piezo acoustic pickup–equipped electric guitar can attest).

You might be thinking, "Why not just pick up a Y splitter cable at Radio Shack?" Well, just because you *can* do something doesn't mean that you *should* do it. You need a hardware box with an isolated transformer to avoid ground loop noise in your amps, and you need the ability to flip the signal out of phase 180 degrees on one of the amp outputs in case running both amps at the same time yields unexpected tone loss while playing. Some switch boxes may provide additional features such as independent gain control for each amp, tuner outputs, MIDI control, and more.

Switching Between More than Two Amps

Don't be afraid to dream big. If you want to switch between many amps, there are some great products that provide this functionality. Be careful about using an audio loop switcher for this purpose, though. Although it seems logical for you to connect multiple loop Sends to the inputs of multiple amps, those products aren't designed to provide a constant load to the Sends when not selected, so functionally, this would be like leaving all of your amps on (not in standby mode) without an instrument cable connected. And you *know* what it sounds like if you connect a cable when the amp is not in standby mode, right? Imagine the damage you would cause to your amps (and your hearing) every time you stepped on a switch to select a different amp!

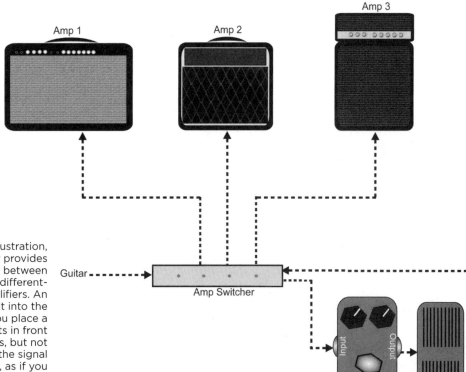

Fig. 4.1: In this illustration, an amp switcher provides instant switching between three very different-sounding amplifiers. An effects loop built into the switcher lets you place a few shared effects in front of all of the amps, but not necessarily in the signal path at all times, as if you just placed them in front of the amp switcher.

Products of Interest: Two-Amp Switching

Lehle Dual SGoS

Fig. 4.2: Lehle
Dual SGoS

The German-made Dual SGoS is perfect for the two-amp rig. It features
A/B/Y operation and has a dedicated Tuner Out, which can alternately be
used to switch between three amps if your rig grows. Other cool features:
polarity switch, independent output-level control, and MIDI remote control.

For simpler needs, the Lehle Little Dual skips the tuner output and
MIDI functions.

Radial Engineering BigShot ABY True Bypass Switcher

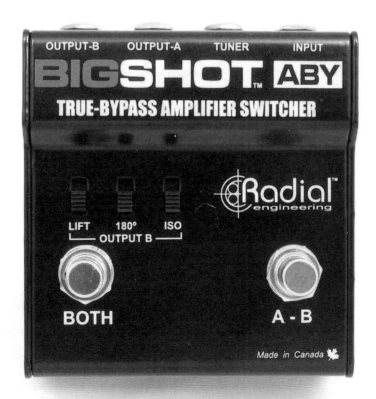

Fig. 4.3: Radial
BigShot ABY

great features as the Lehle Dual SGoS, including a Tuner Out, 180-degree polarity reverse, and an onboard transformer. It doesn't require any power, so it's great for use on a compact pedalboard.

RJM Music Technology Y-Not

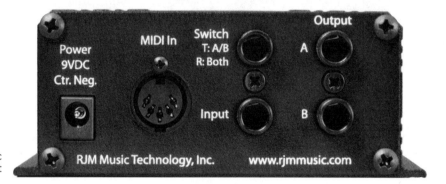

Fig. 4.4: RJM Music Technology Y-Not

The Y-Not is designed to fulfill a few different needs. First, it can switch between two amps (or layer them in typical A/B/Y fashion). But it can also be used to switch between two inputs on one amp! If you've got a classic Fender or Vox amp with independent channels, here's a product designed to give you instant access to both channels without having to constantly swap instrument cables.

The Y-Not has an isolated transformer for the second amp, and features multiple interfaces for remote control. A switching jack lets you select channels via any typical footswitch (or other RJM products), and the Y-Not also has a MIDI interface for easy control from any complex rig.

Other Switch Pedals

There are numerous other switch pedals to consider, including the Tonebone Switchbone, Morley ABY, BOSS LS-2, Framptone Amp Switcher, Electro-Harmonix Switchblade, and the Livewire ABY1.

Products of Interest: Multiple Amp Switching

Radial Engineering JX44 Air Control and JX62 Stage Controls

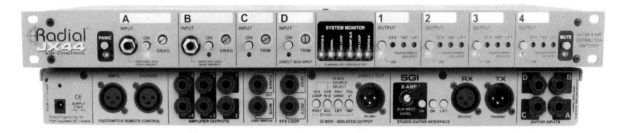

Fig. 4.5: Radial Engineering JX44

For the Radial JX44, switching amps is only the tip of the iceberg. Sure, it can switch between up to four amp rigs (combos/stacks/rack gear), and two of them can be stereo rigs (or you can substitute two *additional* mono amps if needed). But it also enables you to switch between up to four instruments, and advanced features let you optimize levels across the inputs so that you can mix and match instruments with different output levels. This is especially handy when you've got a mix of instruments with active and passive pickups, a DI for your acoustic guitar, and one or more wireless systems.

All of the amps get isolated transformers to avoid ground loops, and you can change polarity as needed on the individual outputs. An effects loop in the JX44 enables you to share effects with all of your amps! If you've ever wondered how to share your compressor and wah pedal with multiple amps, here's your plug-and-play solution.

The fun doesn't stop with a few guitars and amps, however. The JX44 is also an ideal studio tool for recording and re-amping applications. It features a Radial ProDI direct box as well as an X-Amp input for taking a dry guitar signal from your digital audio workstation (DAW) and routing it to your amps for re-amping purposes.

You're probably waiting for me to say, "But wait! There's more!" It's no wonder that so many pros have this box in their rigs. It also has a balanced loop that works with an optional Radial SGI-44 Studio Guitar Interface, enabling you to run a pedalboard up to 300 feet away over balanced XLR cables without adding noise or losing tone. This feature is named for the studio because it also makes it easy to set up your amp in one room while you perform in another location in the studio (like the control room). A tuner output completes the package, and optional footswitches make it easy to select different guitars or different amps on the fly (instead of hitting buttons on the front panel). All that's missing is a MIDI interface. Otherwise, this is a near perfect box for many applications.

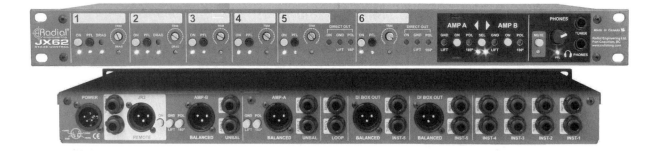

Fig. 4.6: Radial JX62

The new JX62 Stage Control is another fantastic multi-device switcher for both instruments and amplifiers. In this case, the JX62 switches up to six guitars, with the last two instrument inputs featuring Radial direct box outputs for use with acoustic guitars, basses, etc. Each instrument input has a recessed trim control, so you can balance output levels across all of the instruments.

Beyond the six guitar inputs, the JX62 switches between up to two amplifiers, each isolated and phase reversible. An effects loop is inserted between the instrument inputs and the amplifier outputs, so you can share a front-of-amp pedalboard with all of the guitar inputs, and there is also a dedicated tuner output.

Another killer feature for those of you working with a guitar tech in tow: each of the six instrument inputs has a PFL/Tuner switch (pre-fade listen) that mutes an instrument output to everything other than the tuner, so your tech can easily tune instruments without having to re-patch or re-connect anything. There's also a master PFL switch to mute all outputs (other than to the tuner).

In addition to the pair of amplifier outputs, a pair of XLR outputs can either send your acoustic instrument outputs to the front-of-house or connect with the balanced I/O on effects devices like the Axe-FX.

Custom Audio Electronics Amp Selector

Fig. 4.7: CAE Amp Selector

Custom Audio Electronics takes a slightly different approach with its Amp Selector. Whereas the Radial JX44 switches among full rigs, the CAE Amp Selector lets you share a single speaker cabinet (or other load device) between up to four different amps, which can certainly help you reduce your footprint on stage and endear you to your road crew.

Two auxiliary outputs let you send line-level signals to effects and power amps when designing a wet/dry/wet rig, a dedicated tuner output is provided, and the unit features MIDI control! The MIDI interface makes it simple to use other components in your rig to switch between your multiple amps via standard Program Change messages (more details regarding MIDI can be found in Chapter 6).

Voodoo Lab Amp Selector

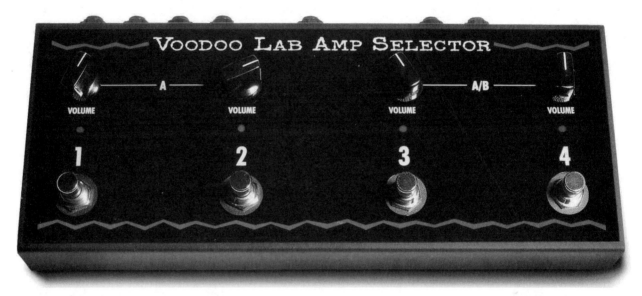

A no-frills utility box on the outside, the Amp Selector fits on your pedalboard and has some great capabilities inside. It lets you switch between up to four amps and up to two guitars, and has a few different modes of operation.

In the default On/Off mode, each button enables or disables the selected amp, which makes it easy to layer sounds from multiple amps at the same time. If you want to instantly switch from one amp to another, the Exclusive mode accomplishes this, and a Single Exclusive mode combines both of these modes in an interesting way: you can activate multiple amps concurrently, but as soon as you step on the button for the Single Exclusive amp, the Amp Selector turns all of the other amp outputs off.

Other features include a dedicated tuner output and operation with stereo amps (two instead of four mono amps).

Fig. 4.8: Voodoo Lab Amp Selector

Guitar Laboratory (G Lab) Line MIDI Switcher LMS-1

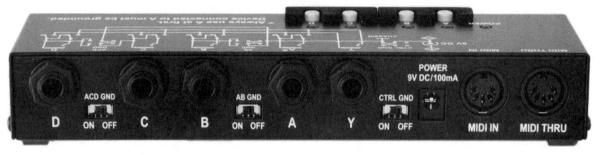

Fig. 4.9: G Lab LMS-1   This compact unit allows you to switch between up to four amps. It's a passive device (so it doesn't offer isolated transformers), but G Lab claims that the shared signal ground avoids ground loop problems.

The LMS-1 can also be used to connect up to four instruments to a single amplifier. And no matter how you want to hook it up, the LMS-1 offers full MIDI control.

Pete Cornish A/B/C Box

This compact pedal enables switching between three amps. In addition to providing isolated outputs and phase reversal on the first two outputs, it also provides balanced outputs to drive long cable lengths from the pedalboard to the amps without noise.

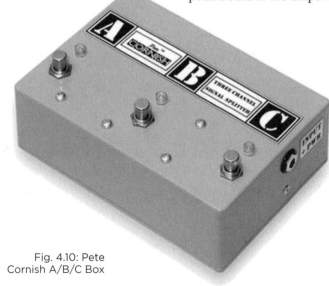

Fig. 4.10: Pete Cornish A/B/C Box

Mesa/Boogie High G

Although it is no longer in production, no discussion of amp switching is complete without talking about this switcher. It accommodates up to four amps, and you'll find it at the heart of many pro rigs today—for good reason. In fact, half of the rigs featured later in this book incorporate this classic switcher.

Besides great audio specs, the HGAS features a shared effects loop, so if you've been wondering how to share one multi-effects processor between multiple amps, you've got an easy solution in this box. It includes standard ¼-inch switching jacks for integration into your rig.

Fig. 4.11: Mesa/Boogie High Gain Amplifier Switcher

CHAPTER 5

Wet/Dry Rigs: Pulling Your Effects Out of the Direct Signal Path

Spend some time in the right online forum and you're bound to hear numerous players talking about wet/dry rigs or wet/dry/ wet rigs. In the pursuit of *ultimate tone*—which can never truly be achieved, of course—wet/dry rigs remove the effects from the guitar's signal path through the amplifier and instead route the output of the effects via a sidechain to one or more additional amps that output your effected (wet) sound.

Wet/Dry Rigs Defined

In a wet/dry rig, you have two amps, each with its own speaker(s)—they can be combos, half stacks, rack gear, whatever. The first amp has your direct (dry) guitar tone and the second amp has the effected tone.

In a wet/dry/wet rig, you have three amps instead of two, each with its own speaker(s). The first amp has your direct (dry) guitar tone, and then the stereo effects returns from your effects are routed to either a stereo rig or two mono rigs. The name wet/dry/wet is commonly used because it describes the typical arrangement of speaker cabinets: left: wet/effects, middle: dry amp, right: wet/effects.

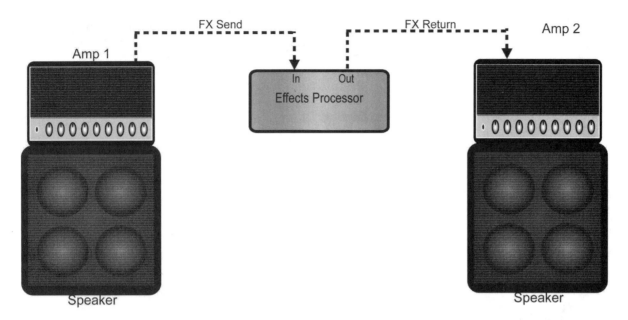

Fig. 5.1: Wet/dry/wet rigs provide incredible tone if the complex setups don't scare you.

The Wet/Dry Advantage: Tone

The advantage of a wet/dry rig is that your guitar tone remains 100 percent pure. It never passes through analog-to-digital conversion in your effects processors, and if you have pedals that color your clean tone, you get the benefit of their effects without any of the negative impact they might otherwise have on your tone.

With your effects routed to a sidechain instead of through your amp along with your dry tone, the wet/dry rig gives you studio-like sound in your live rig. In the recording studio, time-based effects (delay, modulation, reverb) are often added to your tone through the mixing desk or via plug-ins in a digital audio workstation (DAW), which is after your amp has already been miked and recorded to one or more tracks. The effects are placed on a bus and routed to separate tracks (mono or stereo as desired), then blended with your direct guitar tone. The wet/dry rig accomplishes a similar tonal characteristic—blending your effects alongside your direct tone.

If you're tracking guitars in the studio, running a wet/dry rig is essential if you're the kind of tone fanatic who reads a book like this (and if you're not the kind of person who reads a book like this, then we've got some other issues to deal with). If you typically run all of your effects through the effects loop on your amp, it would be extremely bad to find out at mix time that your delay was out of sync with the click track or that your reverb was too loud. You can't properly fix problems with your effects when they're printed to the actual guitar track.

But leaving all of your effects to the producer or mix engineer after the fact doesn't work if effects are an essential part of your sound and style. With a wet/dry rig in the studio, you get to track all of your crazy effects, the mix engineer can mix them independently of your direct tone, and if there's something wrong with your effects, they can be recreated via studio gear or by re-amping your dry guitar parts without having to record new performances.

So even if you run a traditional rig with effects in your loop, when it's time to record, I suggest running your effects in parallel to your main sound via a wet/dry configuration. All it takes is an extra amp with a good-sounding clean channel. If you're used to running a mono guitar rig, keep things simple in your wet/dry configuration and run your effects in mono. Or you can invest a minimal amount of money in a stereo power amp and speaker cabinet to record with stereo effects.

The Wet/Dry Disadvantage: Complexity and Control

With all this greatness, you might think that every serious guitar player would want to run a wet/dry rig. But many of the best guitar players stick to traditional routing of their effects when playing live. The less complex your rig is, the easier it is to troubleshoot when things go wrong. Don't build it big just for bragging rights.

Unfortunately, we learned in the classic *Spider-Man* movie that with great power comes great responsibility, and in the case of a wet/dry rig, that responsibility isn't entirely yours.

In the live setting, your wet amp needs to be miked independently from your dry amp. Who decides on the proper level for your effects? Not you. It's your local neighborhood club soundperson. And his/her idea of your perfect tone may not be the same as your idea of the perfect tone. For example, you love a wet, effected sound, and the soundperson prefers a classic dry guitar tone. If he/she mixes your tone a bit drier than you prefer, you may not have any idea that your front-of-house tone is not the same as your onstage tone.

At the pro touring level, we know of some players who just don't want the front-of-house sound guy having significant control over their tone even when it's their band's personal engineer.

Further, the extra amp and microphones may not be an option at all. If you're one of four bands on a given night with limited setup time and limited space for storing your gear when your band isn't on stage, good luck getting your multi-amp rig set up in time to play. And *extra* good luck getting the house sound engineer to mike your second speaker cabinet for effects, then get the levels set properly. And you were going to ask him to mike that second cabinet in stereo, too, right?

Implementing a Wet/Dry Rig

The ease with which you can implement a wet/dry rig depends on the design of your guitar amp. If you have a parallel effects loop, then the connection is straightforward:

➜ Your amp's Effects Send goes into your multi-effects processor, mixer, or other arrangement of effects.

➜ The mono or stereo output from your effects goes into the input of a mono guitar amp—set to the clean channel—or a stereo power amp.

➜ The output from your wet amp may go to one or more speaker cabinets (or you might be using a combo amp), depending on your preference.

If you have a series effects loop, building a wet/dry rig may be just as easy or a bit more complex, depending on the circuit design. Amp designer Kyle Rhodes of Rhodes Amplification explains: "With a lot of amps, plugging into the Send kills the internal connection to the Return, preventing the use of the Send as a signal. However, in some amps, the Send is always wired to the normalized input of the Return. With this configuration, plugging into the Send does not kill the dry signal through the amp, allowing it to feed a wet effects rig."

Mesa/Boogie amps are typically wired with loops that can be completely hard-bypassed, removing them entirely from the audio circuit. But as a result of this design, patching into the effects loop Send without the Return completely kills the signal. Fortunately, there are a few workarounds. First, these amps commonly feature a Slave Out output, which is a special parallel output that comes *after* the power amp section. This design is useful because you can send this output to your effects loop, and it captures a broader guitar tone than a send from the effects loop, which has all of your preamp tone but none of the power amp tone.

Second, for any amp with this wiring scheme, many times you can use a Y adapter cable to split the signal running through the amp's Effects Send, passing one part of the signal straight back into the Return, and the other part of the signal into your effects. To avoid compromising your tone, though, a cheap Y cable isn't the way to go. A small mixer should be used to turn your series loop into a parallel loop. This will ensure the highest audio quality, and you will have direct control over the wet/dry mix.

Wet Amplifier Considerations

If you run a mono guitar rig, the easiest way to explore building a wet/dry rig is to take a second guitar amp and run the mono output from your effects into the clean channel of this "wet" amp. It might be identical to your primary amp (as is the case with many pro rigs) or it might be something completely different. As this amp is only outputting your wet sound, it doesn't typically have to be as powerful as your primary amp.

Commonly, players will take the stereo output from their effects and run them into a stereo power amp and then into one or more speaker cabinets. Many pro-class 2x12 and 4x12 speaker cabinets are wired for either mono or stereo operation, so oftentimes a stereo cabinet will be used in the wet/dry/wet rig. Using two separate speaker cabinets will give you a broader stereo spread, since you can place the cabinets apart from each other (and as you may recall, wet/dry/wet describes the physical layout of the speaker cabinets in the rig), but you may not want to deal with moving all of that equipment.

Some possible speaker options would be to stack your wet 2x12 cabinet above or below your dry 2x12 or 4x12 cabinet, or if you're running mono effects, use one stereo 4x12 cabinet with the dry signal running to one side of the cabinet and your wet signal to the other side. Each configuration will yield some slightly different-sounding results, but all will deliver a tone that is noticeably different in its response from a traditional rig.

A big source of debate comes up when talking about the stereo power amp. Should this be a tube amp, like you'd use in your traditional guitar rig? I personally like this approach, and if you crave vintage tone from your rig, all tube is a great way to go. You might want to check out some lower-powered tube amps for your wet rig, though, such as models running with EL-84 power tubes instead of the larger EL-34 or 6L6 tubes.

Since your effects will be running in stereo through their own amp, if you have a 50- or 60-watt amp for your dry tone, a stereo power amp that pushes 90 watts per channel might be overkill—and if you're running the wet rig into a 2x12 speaker cabinet, you could end up blowing up a few speakers if you get carried away with the volume, particularly if you're running typical 25- or 30-watt speakers in there. Electro-Voice makes nice 200-watt-rated speakers that are very useful in this particular application if you're making use of a powerful amp and just a pair of speakers. With the effects amp and speaker setup, we're not looking to push the amp into distortion, and we're also not looking to make the speakers break up. Get all that tone goodness from your direct sound in the dry portion of your rig.

There are some players who favor a solid-state power amp like those found in a PA system, and there are even a handful of solid-state, rackmounted, stereo power amps designed for guitar rigs, too. The advantage of solid-state power amps should not be dismissed: their lighter weight might enable you to keep the amp in the same rack as your other gear and not require additional band members for lifting, they generate less heat, and they don't require routine maintenance like tube replacement and biasing. Additionally, some players want a pristine amplification of their effects without the amp imparting its own color to the sound.

However, solid-state amps can make your effects sound like they're coming from . . . a solid-state amp, and not a nice tube amplifier. *The popular thought: if you're using a slave output from your amp, or tapping the signal at the output (many power attenuators feature sidechained outputs that include tone from the power amp section of your head), a solid-state amp is acceptable, since it will just be amplifying your tube amp sound. But if you're routing the signal from the preamp section via an effects loop, run your effects through a guitar or rackmount tube amplifier to maintain the warmth of your tube sound.*

There is a new solution available that straddles both the tube and solid-state worlds: solid-state power amps designed specifically for use in guitar rigs, whether part of a wet/dry rig or powering a modeling amp in the live setting. Check out Chapter 9, "The Compact Rig: Modeling Amps & Profilers," to read about this new breed of power amps from Matrix Amplification.

Chapter 3 highlighted numerous power amps to consider if you want a tube-based guitar amp for your wet sound. If you want a solid-state power amp, a trip to the live sound department of your local music store should reveal numerous options. But don't expect any real advice as to which power amps will sound better or worse in your rig, as those amps were not designed with the guitar player in mind.

CHAPTER 6

MIDI Foot Controllers

Many guitar players often use a combination of rackmounted effects and stomp boxes to create their sounds, and some players take it one step further and include multiple amplifiers and speakers in their guitar rigs, employing a switching system that enables them to access all of their equipment as needed on the fly.

In most cases with complex rigs, MIDI foot controllers are used to control everything from selecting amp channels to switching to different effects. Recently, there has been a resurgence of activity in the design of MIDI foot controllers, and numerous new products exist for the pro guitarist.

MIDI: Your Guitar Rig's Control System

Musical Instrument Digital Interface (MIDI) technology has been used by keyboard players and recording pros since the mid-'80s, but many guitar players still get by without knowing a thing about it. Those low-tech guitarists (dare we call them purists?) won't lose much sleep or go insane trying to figure out the technical stuff, but they also won't be able to create the kinds of sounds you're after for your guitar rig. This chapter isn't for the simple pedal stompers. (But then neither is the rest of this book.)

The MIDI interface of an effects processor is what enables you to change its programs/patches/presets remotely (instead of from the front panel) as well as manipulate many of its settings in real time: turning effect blocks on and off like a stomp box, adjusting parameters such as tremolo speed, reverb depth, tap tempo, and more.

Note: Throughout this chapter, the words programs, patches, *and* presets *are used interchangeably as they each mean the same thing when talking about guitar effects. Although presets is used quite commonly, this should not lead you to assume I'm talking about a factory preset sound created by the manufacturer of your equipment. A preset may be a customized sound that you have saved in your effects processor or amp. I will make use of all of these terms throughout the chapter to get you used to the idea that we're talking about the same thing no matter which word is most familiar to you.*

The MIDI interface on a guitar amp or preamp enables you to switch amp channels (though this can sometimes be done with standard analog switches), and on some of the more advanced guitar preamps, MIDI control can enable you to modify amp settings such as your gain level in real time from a continuous foot controller (think volume pedal) while playing. Whoa! Bringing in your high gain tone by foot while shredding beats having to simplify your performance to roll a guitar's volume knob down and up; plus the sonic results are better overall.

MIDI control of amps and effects merely enables you to change device settings. Your tone can still be all tube, and your effects may still be entirely analog. MIDI is only telling your devices what to do—to change to your heavy-metal shred tone, turn on your Edge-like digital delay, and so on.

Program Change and Continuous Controller Messages

There are only two basic types of MIDI instructions that you'll need to be aware of with guitar gear and foot controllers: Program Change messages and Continuous Controller messages. Other MIDI instruction types exist, like Note Value, but have nothing to do with guitar rigs, as they are used for instructing keyboards to trigger specific notes on a keyboard. If you're doing double duty, playing Moog pedals in a Rush tribute band, however, you may be familiar with some other MIDI commands.

Program Change instructions (or PC messages) are just that—you select a patch number on the foot controller, and it sends a program change instruction to select a specific preset on your rack gear.

A *Continuous Controller* message (or CC message) sends a specific command, typically to turn an effect block on/off, set tap tempo, select a tuner mute/output mute, and more. These are commonly sent from your foot controller when you step on a footswitch. A CC value of 0 or 127 is transmitted, which tells the receiving device to turn an effect on or off.

With an expression pedal (which looks like a volume or wah pedal) connected to a MIDI foot controller, a range of CC values from 0 to 127 is transmitted based on the position of the pedal as you step on it. These might control your amp's volume, where a value of 0 is silent and 127 is whatever your amp's master volume is presently set to, or the expression pedal might be configured to adjust the level of your digital delay repeats. The pedal might control the rate of a vibrato effect, the depth of your chorus, or wild whammy-style pitch effects. You can assign it to different things on a patch-by-patch basis, if desired.

In many MIDI foot controllers, you can set the range of values to be less than the full 0–127, too, so your pedal in its full down position might lower your digital delay effect to 10 percent wet instead of fully off, while the full on position may transmit a maximum CC value of 100 (instead of 127), correlating to the effect being 80 percent wet. And if multiple MIDI instructions can be transmitted simultaneously by your foot controller, one expression pedal might be configured to control different ranges of multiple effects at the same time.

Typically, each MIDI-equipped device listens for instructions on a single MIDI channel (there are 16 channels available), unless it's configured to listen in Omni mode, whereby it will respond to any command it receives on any of the 16 channels. Many MIDI foot controllers can transmit information on multiple MIDI channels concurrently in order to control multiple MIDI devices independently.

By default, all of the MIDI devices you purchase are commonly set to MIDI channel #1, which is why immediately connecting a few pieces of MIDI gear may seem to work sometimes for some basic tasks. Of course nothing may work at all if you bought a used piece of MIDI gear and the previous owner changed the default settings.

Amplifier Considerations

While many guitar players use rackmounted signal processors with rackmounted MIDI-controllable preamps from the likes of Marshall, Mesa/Boogie, ENGL and more, other players are happy to stick with their combos and heads, using the MIDI stuff just for their effects. This is absolutely fine. Really. You don't need my permission to do this, even if I think you're only going halfway to rig heaven.

Many effects processors provide analog switching relays so that you can eliminate the amp's foot controller and change amp channels via the signal processor—just connect an appropriately wired cable or two from the effects processor to the footswitch input jack(s) on the amp/head. With this configuration, you can simultaneously use your MIDI foot controller to switch amp channels and call up new effects programs in your MIDI gear.

For example, using a TC Electronic G-Major, stepping on a MIDI foot controller could send a PC message that calls up your "Screaming Solo" preset #23 in the G-Major, which in turn sends a signal to your amp (via the relay jacks) to switch from its clean channel 1 to its channel 2 for high-gain soloing, rather than having to separately step on the amp's dedicated footswitch independently of your effects.

Today, numerous amps and heads have MIDI functionality built in. You'll find models from ENGL, Hughes & Kettner, Marshall, and more ready to go with MIDI interfaces built in. And fear not—in this book I'll tell you all about the numerous pieces of gear that will let you add MIDI control to any amp.

Making the Connections

To use a MIDI foot controller to change settings on a piece of MIDI equipment, you connect the MIDI Out from the foot controller to the MIDI In of the receiving device, such as your effects processor or preamp.

If you want to control two pieces of MIDI gear, you can connect the MIDI Thru on the first device being controlled to the MIDI In on the second device so that MIDI instructions from your foot controller reach both MIDI devices. Some devices use one combined port labeled Out/ Thru, meaning they both retransmit data from the In port and can generate their own original MIDI data, too.

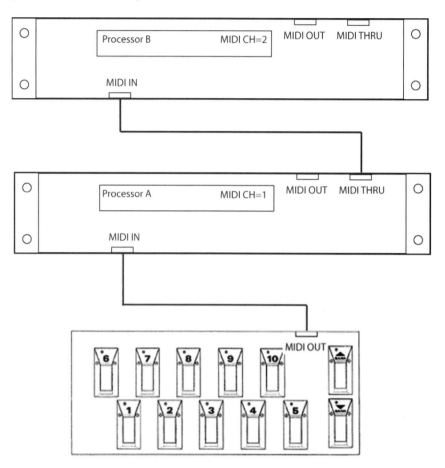

Fig. 6.1: Connecting a MIDI foot controller to one or more effect processors

A MIDI Thru port simply "passes through" all MIDI information that the device receives via its MIDI In port to its MIDI Thru port, sending the original incoming MIDI commands through to the next device's MIDI In port. It's like connecting your foot controller directly to the other piece of MIDI equipment . . . almost.

Latency is the term that describes the delay of an electrical signal—not a good kind of delay, like with your digital effects, but rather a delay in the time it takes for an electrical signal to travel from one place to another. If there is too much latency introduced by the first device you've connected to your foot controller, you could experience an audible delay when changing settings on the second device in your MIDI chain. This could be incredibly inconvenient. For example, imagine kicking in your lead solo sound only to find your amp channel switching a few milliseconds too late . . . after you already started soloing while still on your clean tone!

If you plan to control your entire rig from a single MIDI foot controller, make your guitar preamp the first piece of equipment in the MIDI signal chain, followed by any effect processors. It's more important to be able to instantly switch your amp channel than to switch your flanger effect on or off.

Although you don't have to make the reverse connection from your preamp/effect processor's MIDI Out to your foot controller's MIDI In (requiring a second MIDI cable), sometimes it can be useful. We'll look at this connection option in greater detail later in this chapter.

Power to the Pedal

MIDI foot controllers must be connected to a power source, typically via traditional "wall warts" or an internal power supply or battery source. If the idea behind having a MIDI controller was to minimize cables on the floor, you'll be excited to learn about a popular foot controller feature called *phantom power* that enables you to power your pedalboard through your MIDI cable.

Usually, phantom power is supplied by a special 7-pin DIN MIDI cable. Traditional MIDI cables have 5-pin DIN connectors, but a few clever manufacturers realized that two additional pins in a 7-pin cable could be used to supply power in the cable alongside your MIDI data.

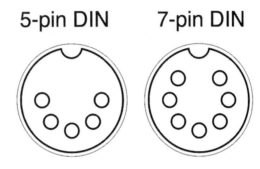

Fig. 6.2: Standard MIDI interfaces

In devices equipped with a 7-pin DIN jack, you can still typically use standard 5-pin MIDI cables and external power sources.

Yet just because your foot controller supports phantom power isn't enough reason to rejoice—you still need a power source at the other end of the cable to actually supply the current. Some devices have a power supply that can supply phantom power internally, but other devices (for example, certain guitar preamps like the Mesa/Boogie Triaxis) have a phantom power input jack on the rear of the unit. You take the MIDI foot controller's original power supply/wall wart and plug it into the back of the preamp, and power is passed through from the power input jack to the foot controller.

While this may seem odd, it ensures that you're able to supply the correct voltage to the foot controller without any issues. And since we're dealing with rackmounted equipment, you just plug the wall wart into the back of your rackmounted line conditioner. You have one of those, right?

If you have a preamp or effects processor that is capable of supplying phantom power, I highly recommend using a foot controller that takes advantage of this great feature.

A few foot controllers can receive phantom power on a standard 5-pin DIN cable as well, but this is not the norm, and can lead to other challenges:

→Because MIDI signals traditionally only used three of the five pins (two for data and one for ground), to save money on manufacturing, some companies historically sold cheap MIDI cables that didn't have all five pins wired, rendering their use in this scenario impossible.

→You can't glance at the 5-pin DIN MIDI connector on a piece of equipment and automatically know whether it supports phantom power.

If you end up with a 7-pin DIN foot controller and a 5-pin DIN piece of rack gear that supports phantom power, some custom cables and adapters may enable you to connect the products and take advantage of the phantom power capability (Rocktron makes one such cable that even lets you connect a power supply at the 5-pin DIN end when you don't actually have a piece of rack gear capable of supplying power). If you're handy with custom wiring and a soldering gun, you can custom-wire your own cable with a 5-pin DIN at one end and a 7-pin DIN at the other.

Fig. 6.3: The Rocktron MIDI cable can provide phantom power convenience while also handling the 5-pin to 7-pin difference.

XLR MIDI: The Emerging Non-Standard Standard

Many of the leading professional rig infrastructure companies (like RJM Music Technology, Mark L Custom Audio, Skrydstrup R&D, etc.) have embraced what is commonly referred to as XLR MIDI: using XLR cables to carry MIDI data and power between foot controllers and racks rather than using 7-pin DIN MIDI cables. The XLR cables feature more robust connectors and can typically run greater distances. If you have a switching system in your rig and a MIDI foot controller from the same manufacturer, these cable solutions work great.

First, let's dispel the misconception you already have about the interface: this is not a 3-pin XLR microphone cable! The outside casing is the same form factor as your familiar microphone XLR connector, but there are actually six pins in these connectors.

The trouble you'll run into—a minor annoyance, really—is that there is no formal standard for MIDI data transmission over anything but a 5-pin DIN MIDI connector. Most of the companies using XLR MIDI have different pin-outs on their equipment, so if you were to connect an RJM Music

Technology MIDI foot controller to a Mark L audio looper/switcher with a cable from either company, the products wouldn't function correctly (if at all).

Fortunately, the manufacturers openly publish their wiring specs, so anyone with experience wiring custom cables could build you the proper cable that has one manufacturer's pin-outs at one end and the other manufacturer's pin-outs at the other. I had no trouble using a Mark L FC-25 MIDI foot controller with an RJM Music Rack Gizmo over an XLR MIDI cable once I supplied RJM Music Technology with the proper pin-outs and ordered a custom-wired cable.

Keep in mind that most of these manufacturers also support 7-pin DIN MIDI connections on their devices in addition to the XLR MIDI interfaces, and that interface tends to operate universally on these products.

Alternate Hookup Considerations

Using a single MIDI controller to change settings on your preamp and one or two (or more) signal processors can make the programming of your MIDI setup quite complex.

Depending on your playing style, it might be better to use two separate foot controllers—one for your amp and another for your effects. If you have a guitar amp head/combo with its own footswitch for channel switching, don't feel like you have to give that up and surrender control of your amp to your MIDI setup. There are many old-school players who like to do things manually, but crave the fantastic sound of rack-based effects processors. As you'll see in our rig examples, Rush guitarist Alex Lifeson has a rig capable of fully automatic control, but he prefers to do a pedal tap dance. Clearly, it doesn't hurt his playing.

Having used numerous MIDI setups over the years, there are a few instances when I prefer to use two separate foot controllers for my amp and my effects. Although my guitar preamp could be controlled by the same foot controller that is attached to my effects processor, this approach requires careful planning of program changes as they relate to settings on my amp/preamp.

With my amp/preamp controlled independently by its own foot controller, I can leave one particular effects setup in place and change between clean and distorted channels in the amp while the effects remain constant. This is particularly convenient when composing new music or just jamming for fun—I can randomly dial up programs in my effects processor and easily switch individual effects on or off from one foot controller and, with my other footswitch, select various clean or overdriven sounds in my guitar preamp. If you're exploring hundreds of presets in a new multi-effects processor, this setup is highly advantageous, as you can call up one effect and then audition how it sounds with your various clean and overdriven amp tones.

But once you're past the exploring phase and are ready to hit the road on a tour with a well-defined set list, it makes more sense to use a single foot controller and save presets with the appropriate combination of effects and amp channels.

Finding the Best Approach Before You Start

Before setting up your MIDI-fied rig, you should decide which approach to device control best suits your needs—make this your first decision. Depending on the approach you take, it will require more or less programming either in your effects processors or in your foot controller(s). *You can't figure this out halfway through hooking up your devices!* And yes, you should plan to invariably make the wrong choice first and have to redo things later. But that's just part of the voyage of discovery!

Programming Logic: In Your Foot Controller or in Your Effects?

Let's assume that you have two MIDI-controllable effects processors—perhaps a dedicated reverb/delay unit and a general-purpose multi-effects processor. When you step on a specific pedal, you would like Processor A to switch to preset #36 and Processor B to select preset #27. This simple event can be interpreted by your equipment in a few different ways.

We'll assume that both devices are set to the same MIDI channel, or Omni mode, and you've made MIDI connections like the example seen in Fig. 6.1. By default, your foot controller sends a single program change value on a single MIDI channel. There is a one-to-one mapping of these numbers, so if your foot controller was in its first bank of presets and you stepped on button #3, your controller would typically send a PC message on MIDI channel 1 to your effects processors, telling them to call up program/patch/preset #3. We say *typically*, because sometimes the numbers don't line up.

With computer-controlled devices, sometimes program/patch numbering begins with #1, but in some devices, the first program is #0. Stepping on button #1 will call up program #0, button #2 will call up program #1, and so on, until you reprogram either the foot controller or the preamp/processor. Some foot controllers have a built-in feature to select whether program changes begin at #0 or #1—a very handy feature, while some multi-effects processors have a feature to change how they respond to incoming PC message numbering.

You have some decisions to make for processing patch changes within your effects processors:

➜ You could just save a copy of presets #36 and #27 in your effects processors to preset location #3 in each (the example above), or any number that you call up from the foot controller. This is the simplest approach, which requires no programming work in your foot controller, but you'll end up overwriting tons of great-sounding effects patches in your equipment with duplicates. *I do not recommend this approach for most players. If you choose this option, I'm going to take your rack away and trade you a set of secondhand stomp boxes.*

➜ By using the MIDI Mapping function in your effects processor or rack preamp, you can change how it responds to a PC message. For example, when Processor A receives a PC command, you can set it so that incoming PC message #3 sets the processor to patch #36. You can save customized MIDI maps for all of the program locations in your processors. You can even use the mapping feature to shift your program changes by one if you're experiencing the zero/one numbering issue mentioned earlier.

I don't know of many popular MIDI-controlled preamps or effects processors that lack this simple capability. *Learn to use the MIDI mapping feature of your effects processor(s), because it is one of the simplest ways to choose the right patches with a single PC message sent by your MIDI foot controller.*

→Many foot controllers can be programmed to send one or more program changes on multiple MIDI channels concurrently. Some can also be programmed to handle your MIDI mapping simultaneously. For example, stepping on pedal #3 could be configured in the foot controller to send PC value #36 on MIDI channel #1 *and* value #27 on MIDI channel #2. You don't have to have a direct correlation between the button numbers on your foot controller and the effect settings in your rig.

Sending program changes on multiple MIDI channels is very convenient if you have two or three devices under the control of your pedalboard, but it introduces the requirement of learning to program your foot controller. You will also need to spend some time thinking about which patches you want to call up in your effects processor(s) on a song-by-song basis, and then map them out on paper in order to facilitate programming the foot controller with minimal frustration. *It is typically easier to program and review MIDI mappings in your individual MIDI-controlled devices than it is to program or review these settings in most foot controllers.*

Continuous Controllers: Adding Pedals to Your Pedals

Just because the MIDI foot controller you're interested in purchasing doesn't have a built-in continuous controller doesn't mean you can't add one (or more) to it.

Many foot controllers have input jacks for connecting one or more pedals of various types—continuous controllers for adjusting everything from volume to wah effects to tremolo speed to delay repeats and more, plus additional switch pedals for single-function on/off tasks such as dedicated tap tempo control, switching to your tuner output, and gain boosts for soloing, to name a few. The more versatile the MIDI capabilities of your foot controller, the more options you'll have for controlling your rack gear.

You'll want at least one continuous controller in your setup, and with pedal input jacks on your foot controller, you'll have the opportunity to select specific pedals with just the right feel instead of settling for whatever continuous controller is built into your foot controller. Some players prefer a wah pedal that is spring-loaded, while others prefer the feel of a traditional volume pedal.

Whatever your preference, you'll usually have the option to add either a dedicated continuous controller pedal (like the popular Roland EV-5 Expression Pedal) or, in many cases, you can use a volume pedal for MIDI control. Connections are made either with ¼-inch stereo cables or with insert cables that have a ¼-inch stereo connection at one end and two

¼-inch mono cables at the other. Because these Y cables are frequently used for connecting rackmounted processors like compressors and noise gates to mixing consoles, you'll find them in the recording audio section of your favorite music store.

No audio signal is ever passed into or through a volume pedal used for expression pedal purposes—only the output jack is connected to your foot controller, and this is only used to generate changes in electrical current that are translated by the foot controller into MIDI CC values in the 0–127 range for controlling a specified effect in your rack gear. So don't waste money on a premium cable for this purpose—it doesn't impact your tone at all!

Are You Latching Onto All of This?

Bad pun aside, the pedals in MIDI foot controllers are either Momentary, Latching, or adjustable through programming.

Momentary pedals send one MIDI value when stepped on (typically CC value 127) and another value (typically CC value 0) when released. Latching pedals are pure on/off transmitters . . . the first time you hit them, they send a value of 127 (On), and the next time they send a value of 0 (Off).

Your effects processor(s) may react in unexpected ways if it receives an invalid CC message created by using an inappropriate type of pedal. Adjusting Tap Tempo usually works best with a Latching pedal because the effects processor typically waits for two full press/release actions with the pedal to establish a tempo. If you hit a Momentary pedal once for setting Tap Tempo, it will register your tempo as being the difference in time from when you first depressed the pedal to the time you released the pedal, which is not going to generate the tempos you had in mind for your delay repeats or other synchronized sound effects.

When setting up your MIDI foot controller, it's important to figure out what kind of pedal response your effects processor is configured to work with, and then make sure that your floor controller is configured to match.

The Lights Are On (or Off), but Is Anyone Home?

With all-in-one floor-based effects such as the Boss GT-10, TC Electronic Nova System, or Line 6 POD HD Pro when you select a patch, you see lights on the foot controller identifying which effect blocks are active—chorus, delay, reverb, compressor, etc. Unfortunately, with MIDI foot controllers connected to rack gear, it's not as simple as making the reverse connection of a MIDI Out from your processor to the MIDI In of your foot controller. Typically, the result of this connection is . . . absolutely nothing, because manufacturers never agreed on a specific way to handle these effect block status messages when they drafted the MIDI specifications.

In order for most foot controllers to display the On/Off status of effect blocks when a new preset is called up, they need to receive MIDI instructions from your rack gear, and this requires a second MIDI cable. However, there is no standard protocol within the MIDI specification for transmitting effect block status. Therefore, depending on the foot controller and rack gear you have, a second MIDI cable is often unnecessary because there is no additional functionality gained. Furthermore, some foot controllers store effect block status in their internal memory, which also negates the need for more than a single MIDI cable.

Even with a single MIDI cable, you are still able to control the On/Off status of effect blocks manually via CC messages, and if your foot controller has LEDs associated with each button, they will light up on the foot controller when you step on them to change a pedal state from Off to On.

Unfortunately, when you first load a program/patch/preset, your foot controller has no idea what the status of each effect block is within a patch, so all of your effect block status buttons are visually off on the foot controller by default, even if the preset you selected had some of those blocks enabled at the time.

You can see the problem quite easily. Imagine that you select a preset in your TC Electronic G-Major that has chorus and delay effect blocks on, but all of the effect blocks appear to be off by default on your Ground Control Pro MIDI foot controller when you first select the patch. The first time you step on the footswitch for controlling the status of the chorus effect block, the foot controller sends a MIDI CC instruction to the G-Major to turn the effect block on. Maybe your effects processor ignores this and the foot controller turns on the light for that switch, and the next time you step on the pedal, the effect is turned off and the corresponding LED turns off as well. But, more commonly, your effects processor turns the chorus effect off and the foot controller illuminates the switch, so now it appears that your chorus effect is on, but it's actually in the opposite state. Yikes!

Option 1: The simplest but not so elegant solution is to program different effect presets/patches for all of your necessary effect states instead of turning effect blocks on/off within a patch. For example, program #41 in your G-Major is saved with your chorus, delay, and reverb on by default, and program #42 has only the chorus and reverb, but no delay. You can then change the state of each effect without regard for the illuminated status of each pedal by simply selecting different effect presets from your foot controller. But no self-respecting MIDI-enabled guitarist would do this unless he had no choice, like in Maddi Schieferstein's horror story when John Petrucci's foot controller died while on tour in Mexico (see sidebar).

Option 2: With most professional MIDI foot controllers, you can easily program the default state of individual buttons to correspond to your effects. In this scenario, when you select program #12 from your G-Major containing the chorus and delay effect blocks set to "on" from your foot controller, you also save a corresponding patch selection in your foot controller with those effect block footswitches set to their "on" state by default. It's usually a very simple process to make this change on the foot controller. But this requires some planning on your part since you have to first create effects patches the way you want them, then program the foot controller, and then . . . don't change things! Every time you change the configuration of one of your presets, you'll have to remember to go back and reprogram your foot controller to match if you've changed the default state of an effect block status.

Dedicated Solutions

Thankfully, dedicated solutions do exist that overcome this technical burden and behave like all-in-one floor-based effect boxes. With the TC Electronic G-System, a Fractal Audio Axe-FX paired with its MFC-101 foot controller, Line 6 POD HD Pro and matching Line 6 pedalboard, or even some older (but still popular) products like Lexicon's MPX-G2 effects processor with a Lexicon R1 foot controller, effect block status is ready the moment you select a new preset.

It should be noted, however, that the G-System and Line 6 pedalboards are not MIDI foot controllers in the truest sense of the term. These foot controllers connect via proprietary methods to the effects units, and then those devices (the POD X3 Pro or G-System GFX-01 brain) have MIDI jacks for connecting to additional devices. But this proprietary connection is what makes it especially easy for these foot controllers to properly display effects status.

Some MIDI foot controllers have been preprogrammed to provide the correct visual information for specific effects processors, typically from the same manufacturer as the foot controller, but sometimes for popular processors from other manufacturers. If the effects processor transmits effect block status in its set of MIDI instructions, then a generic foot controller can be designed to properly interpret those proprietary instructions.

MIDI Disaster in Mexico: Tale from the Trenches

As told to me by Matt "Maddi" Schieferstein, guitar tech and rig builder for Dream Theater's John Petrucci:

We were doing the G3 tour in South America in 2012. John had decided to go back to using the Mesa/Boogie Triaxis and 2:Ninety power amp for the tour. I had built a compact rig using the Triaxis/2:Ninety, Axe-FX II, and a small set of pedals for front-end effects. Everything was MIDI controlled from an Axess Electronics FX-1 controller. We have used those FX-1s for years with several of John's guitar rigs, and they are built like tanks.

We had arrived in Mexico City for the last two shows. The rig had worked flawlessly all through South America. After loading into the venue, I set the rig up and connected all of the cabling. When I powered the rig on, I saw that the FX-1 was not powering on correctly. Normally, when you power an FX-1 on, it goes through an LED test and screen check. To my surprise, mine did none of that.

After some troubleshooting and speaking to Mario from Axess, we determined that the FX-1 was not going to be fixed that day. My next move was to call John at the hotel and fill him in on what was happening. After the call, I got busy trying to find a MIDI foot controller . . . As I found out, that's not the easiest thing to find in Mexico. I first went to the promoter and asked if any local bands might have one that we could borrow for the two shows.

While the promoters were checking their sources, I called Voodoo Lab to see if there was a dealer in Mexico City to try and get a Ground Control Pro. That seemed to be the best option for the rig. After getting the distributor's phone number in Mexico, I called and found out that they did in fact have one in stock. The only snag was it was located at their warehouse in Monterey . . . that's about a ninety-minute plane ride from Mexico City. The distributor said to me on the phone, "If you pay for it right now through our website, I will take it to the airport and get it on a plane to Mexico City. But I can't guarantee it will make the flight or get there today." I said, "Okay, let's make it happen," and the deal was done.

While I was on the phone with the distributor, the promoter told me they found a pedalboard with MIDI that we could borrow. Great! At least we could get through soundcheck and the show if the Ground Control Pro didn't arrive. Imagine the look on my face when a kid showed up with an ART X-11. Yes, the black and neon pink foot controller from the late '80s . . .

Well, that controller presented its own set of issues as I tried to interface it with a slightly more modern rig. As you know, the X-11 can only do patch changes. There is no way to access or control individual effects via CC changes. So I ended up building five presets (Clean/Crunch/Crunch Chorus/Lead 1/Lead 2) in the Axe-FX with just the effects needed. It was not the best option, but we got through soundcheck and were ready to get through the show.

At this point, I have to say John was a champ. About thirty minutes before Steve Lukather went on, the Ground Control Pro arrived! I took it to the dressing room along with the programming notes I had made earlier in the day and configured the Ground Control Pro. John looked up and asked if we were going to use it for the show. "Yes we are!" I replied.

Without any time to test and troubleshoot in advance, I took it to the stage, hooked it up, and everything worked!

Fig. 6.4: If you plan to use your foot controller to send CC messages, it's essential that you label the pedals!

Which One Should I Buy?

Due to the specialized audience that MIDI foot controllers serve, you will not find many of them (if any) at your local guitar shop. In fact, most popular controllers are only available directly from their respective manufacturers or from specialty shops.

While the best advice with many products is to "try before you buy," you rarely have that opportunity with this kind of product, so your purchasing decision will most likely be based on your evaluation of the products from online information, product specifications, and reviews (MusicPlayers.com has in-depth reviews of many MIDI foot controllers).

→First determine your pedal needs, and then see if an available product meets or exceeds that need. If a foot controller only enables you to switch three effect blocks on and off, but your processor features six switchable effect blocks, that foot controller may be too limited for your rig.

→Do you prefer to control your effects stomp-box style or would you rather select preprogrammed patches on your processor? Different foot controllers use different methods of sending PC commands and CC messages. Some have separate pedals for each of these functions, while others have one set of shared pedals and a mode-change switch that toggles between these operating modes. Does the foot controller you're considering enable you to make changes as rapidly as you'll need to?

Products of Interest: MIDI Foot Controllers

There are numerous MIDI foot controllers on the market, and I haven't even begun to cover half of them here. What follows are some very brief descriptions of popular models designed with the pro musician in mind. If I were to go into the specifications for how many MIDI messages of each type are sent by every pedal, this would definitely become the "now I lay me down to sleep" chapter.

Each of these foot controllers has switches (commonly the bottom row, but sometimes user assignable) that can be used for preset selection and other instant-access switches for directly turning effects on/off or sending other MIDI CC messages as needed.

Custom Audio Electronics RS-10 and RST-V

Fig. 6.5: Custom Audio Electronics RS-10

Bob Bradshaw's CAE has been building this stuff longer than everyone, and his RS-10 foot controller is one of the most widely used in big rigs. A more compact RS-5 is also available. Shown here with an expansion module that provides six additional instant-access switches and two additional preset buttons, its straightforward design, ability to send multiple messages on multiple channels concurrently, and solid construction keep players of all calibers flocking to it. Unfortunately, the lack of a meaningful display keeps other players from being excited about it. If you're one of those players, fear not and keep reading!

Multiple units can be connected to each other for control from multiple points on- or offstage. Although built with other CAE loopers, switchers, and mixers in mind, it works great with any rig you decide to build.

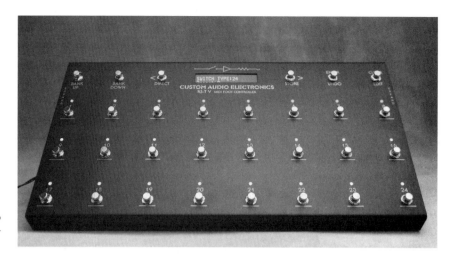

Fig. 6.6: Custom Audio
Electronics RS-T 24

Introduced in 2011 were the RS-T 24 and the base unit RS-T. The obvious feature upgrade is a new two-line alpha-numeric display, and less obvious from this photo are the multicolored LEDs, which can be assigned to represent different functions; for example, blue for presets and red for instant-access switches.

Switches are fully configurable for operation, so there's no need to worry about having a set number of switches for instant-access functions or preset selections. MIDI capabilities have been expanded significantly over the older controllers, too. The RS-T V can send more MIDI commands from a single button push than I imagine anybody could ever need!

Four expression pedal inputs and a pair of 9V DC outlets for powering a handful of pedals on the floor enhance this already great update.

Guitar Laboratory GSC-5

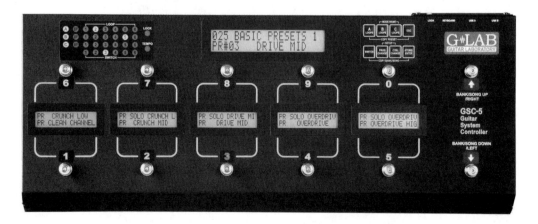

Fig. 6.7: G Lab GSC-5   Designed as part of a larger family of products, the G Lab GSC-5 has storage space beneath the surface for installing modules specific to your needs, including floor-based audio loops, a universal pedal power supply, amp switching, and more.

The unique set of displays provides a fantastic amount of visual feedback regarding your sounds, and a matrix at the top shows information such as which loops are enabled. Programming the unit is made easy thanks to the inclusion of a very compact, lightweight dedicated USB keyboard, complete with custom buttons specific to configuring the GSC-5. Cool stuff!

Skrydstrup SC-1

Fig. 6.8: Skrydstrup SC-1

The SC-1 is an expandable unit similar to the CAE RS-10, but its 12-character display and secondary numeric display up the ante by providing meaningful information such as custom names for your presets. Taking things over the top is an included software editor that makes it simple to program the unit and create custom set lists.

RJM Music Technology MasterMind GT

Fig. 6.9: RJM MasterMind GT

If you're thinking that this must be one of the most sophisticated MIDI foot controllers ever created, you would be correct, as the MasterMind GT does pretty much everything you want a foot controller to do, and it makes both configuration and operation a breeze, thanks to a combination of great hardware and software.

RJM Music Technology products are typically among the easiest to configure of any products on the market, and Ron Menelli went over the top with this design. The obvious difference between the MasterMind GT and every other MIDI foot controller is its amazing user interface. Gone are the days of taping labels to your switches. Each button can be configured to perform any function, so if you want bank-select switches in the top row or two, instant access switches on the bottom row, tap tempo a few buttons over from the left or assigned to the bottom middle, you can do that. Or you can put your familiar patch selection buttons on the bottom one or two rows and assign instant access switches above. Once you've assigned buttons, you can create custom labels—names and colors—that make it easy for you to understand the operation of your rig.

Because there are multiple displays, configuring your rig from the hardware itself is easier than with most foot controllers. When editing your setup, different functions/options appear on each of the displays, so you don't need to scroll through multiple menus with cryptic instructions limited by a basic LCD display. But even this isn't easy enough for me, so I opt to use RJM's software-based editor on my MacBook when it's time for configuring a custom set list or simply reprogramming my rig operation.

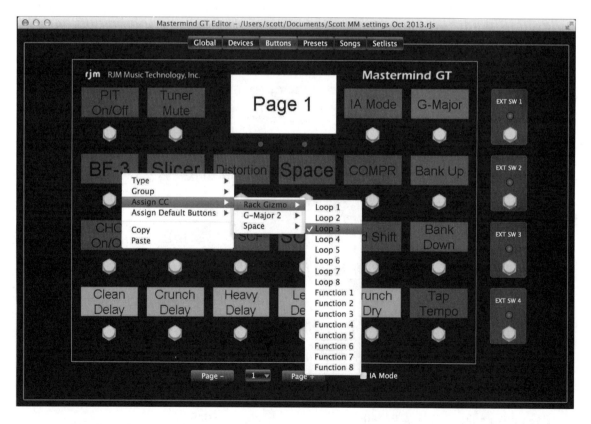

Fig. 6.10: The MasterMind GT's software editor makes programming your effects and set lists even easier than the great hardware interface already accomplishes.

The MasterMind GT ships preconfigured with templates for controlling numerous popular products, including the Axe-FX, G-Major 2, and some Eventide Factor/Space pedals, and when paired with an RJM function switcher or audio looper, it can be powered via an XLR MIDI cable (familiar 7-pin DIN phantom power is also provided).

A new, more compact, 10-button version of the MasterMind GT is also available.

Fig. 6.11: RJM Mastermind GT/10

Axess Electronics FX-1

Fig. 6.12: Axess Electronics FX-1

You've seen the FX-1 in front of many guitar heroes. One feature that's hard to see from the photo is the size: it's big, with three inches of space between each button, making it easy for you to use even if you perform wearing boots.

Besides the common features you expect of products like the FX-1, it can be chained with multiple units on- and offstage, and it includes a software editor to make configuring your presets and set lists easy. It can also be expanded with the FX-1 Expander module, which adds twelve more instant-access switches.

TC Electronic G-System

Fig. 6.13: TC Electronic
G-System

The G-System is a product that has had a revolutionary impact on the world of pro guitar rigs. In one unit, you get a fantastic-sounding multi-effects processor that includes four true-bypass pedal loops, amp channel switching, and a gorgeous MIDI foot controller that provides great visual feedback.

The brains of the unit, seen below, can be mounted in your rack for easy connection to the rest of your rig, and then a single RJ-45 Ethernet cable is all that it takes to connect the foot controller up to 49 feet away. Your volume and expression pedal can attach directly to the foot controller, or to the rackmounted GFX01, or you can attach pedals in both locations. It's always handy to have a secondary wah pedal location on a platform above the drum kit for crazy soloing, right?

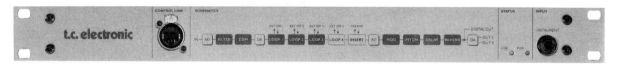

Fig. 6.14: TC
Electronic GFX01
can be rackmounted
when removed
from underneath
the G-System foot
controller.

The G-System doesn't have as detailed an implementation of MIDI commands as some of the other dedicated products described here, but if you have straightforward requirements for PC and CC messages, controlling a few external pedals, etc., it's hard to beat this winning package. Psicraft Design's free Vyzor Editor makes configuration even easier than using the already easy-to-use hardware interface, and the sidebar describes an example of integrating the G-System with some other popular tools for fully automated rig control.

Controlling a Complex Rig with the TC Electronic G-System, RJM Music Technology RG-16, and a Multi-Channel Amp

The TC Electronic G-System really shines once you start customizing its functionality a bit. Here's one example of how I integrated it into a rig:

The RJM Music Technology RG-16 provides amp channel and function switching, plus its own set of eight pedal loops, and the device is easily MIDI controlled. When connected to my Mesa/Boogie Road King II head, the RG-16 (or the Amp Gizmo, which is the same basic device sans audio loops) can switch among most of the amp's enormous range of switching options—four channels, two effects loops, Reverb, and Solo/Boost. This is certainly more than most switching options cover, plus the G-System can't switch four channels on a modern Mesa/Boogie amplifier due to differences in how the switching jacks are wired.

MIDI Out from the G-System was connected to the MIDI In on the RJM RG-16, and a custom RJM cable was connected from the RG-16 to the Road King II's input jack where a King Controller footswitch would typically be attached.

For soloing, I prefer to use the Solo feature in my Mesa/Boogie head rather than a simple decibel boost/cut approach within the G-System, so I easily changed the operation of the G-System's Boost pedal to send a MIDI Continuous Controller (CC) message that corresponded to that function in the RG-16 rather than activating the G-System's internal volume boost. With this change, stepping on the G-System's Boost pedal activates the Solo/Boost feature in the amp instead of changing the G-System's internal signal level.

But I didn't stop there. Despite the inclusion of some fantastic digital reverbs in the G-System, I have a fondness for my amp's analog reverb. Just as easily as before, I changed the Reverb button's functionality to send a CC message to the RG-16 rather than activating the internal reverb effect. Stepping on the Reverb button then activated the reverb built into the amp, thanks to the RG-16. The entire solution above would have worked exactly the same with the RJM Amp Gizmo instead of the RG-16, since it didn't involve use of the audio loops.

In one of my other rigs, I only ran the G-System in the effects loop of my preamp, and I relied upon another RG-16 to provide pedal loops in front of the preamp's input for a few pedal effects. In this wiring scenario, all of the G-System loops would end up post-input instead of pre. I assigned the buttons on the G-System for its Loops 1, 2, and 3 to MIDI CC values so that stepping on them sent a command to the RG-16 to activate those audio loops instead of the loops in the G-System. All of this was accomplished with simple point-and-click changes within the Vyzor software editor.

Voodoo Lab Ground Control Pro

Fig. 6.15: Voodoo Lab Ground Control Pro

The Ground Control Pro has been one of the most popular foot controllers on the market for a long time. It features a familiar assortment of instant-access and preset selection switches, inputs for continuous controllers, and phantom power. The display is large enough to provide descriptive names of your presets, and programming from the floor unit is reasonably easy once you get used to the interface.

Mark L Custom Guitar Electronics FX-25 and FC-25

Fig. 6.16: Mark L FX-25

With a slightly different arrangement of buttons and the ability to send a dizzying array of commands simultaneously from a single pedal, the FX-25 is different enough from other professional foot controllers to stand out. Even without the optional expansion module(s), there are twelve instant access switches above six preset selection buttons. The older FC-25 is functionally identical but is slightly larger (longer).

Fig. 6.17: The Mark L FX25 MIDI foot controller can be expanded with up to two expanders for even more instant access and preset selection footswitches.

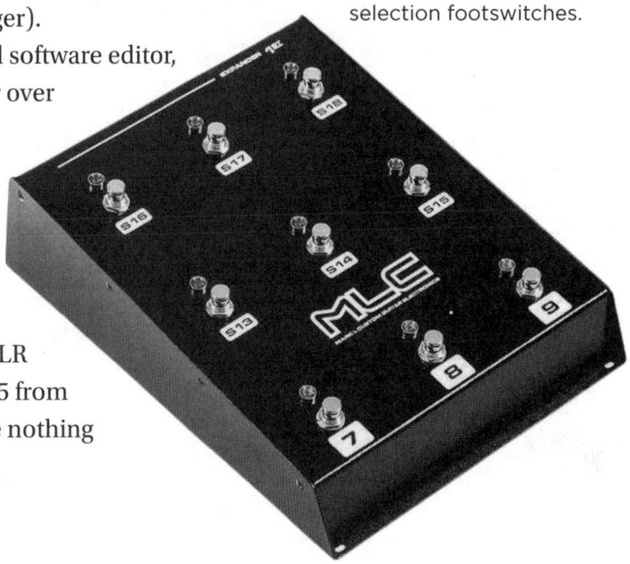

The unit is easily configured via an included software editor, and although it doesn't accept phantom power over 7-pin DIN, Mark L foot controllers can receive power from Mark L switchers/loopers via XLR MIDI (or the included 9V AC power supply). A nice touch is that the FX-25 provides 9V DC power for your wah and tuner pedals. After studying the pin-outs, I had RJM Music Technology wire for me a custom XLR MIDI cable that enabled me to power the FC-25 from my Rack Gizmo. It worked perfectly, and I have nothing but praise for this foot controller.

Rhodes M/21: Machine MIDI Foot Controller

The M/21 was designed to control other Rhodes Amplification products. If you have one of the company's audio loopers or amplifiers, the M/21 gives you direct control over loops and amp settings in addition to sending typical PC and CC messages for controlling your other MIDI gear.

Fig. 6.18: Rhodes Amplification M/21

With the large OLED graphics display and uniquely spaced buttons, control of your effects is easy (switches are staggered so it's easier to hit the top row of buttons without accidently stepping on the front row). There are some other clever features, such as automatic preset selection via expression pedal activity and built-in tap-tempo storage and recall within each preset.

Rocktron All Access Limited

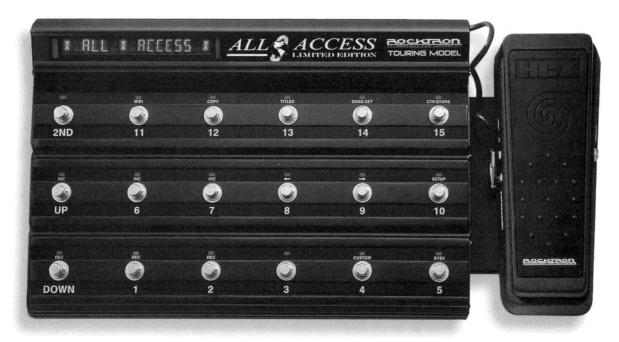

Fig. 6.19: Rocktron
All Access Limited

Similar to the Ground Control Pro, the All Access Limited differs from the standard All Access only in its black instead of silver coloring and the inclusion of a matching continuous controller pedal.

In addition to the familiar options for banks of presets and instant-access pedals, these foot controllers have integrated support when used with Rocktron effects processors and preamps, sharing display information from the rack units with the foot controller's display.

Fig. 6.20: Fractal
Audio MFC-101

Fractal Audio Systems MFC-101

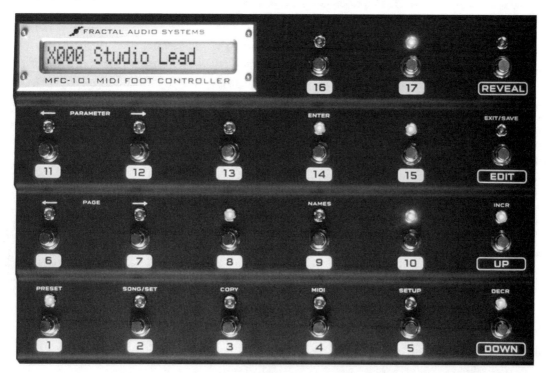

Designed for program-free operation with Fractal Audio's Axe-FX effects processor and amp modeler, the MFC-101 also works as a universal MIDI foot controller with all the typical expected features: a large, easy-to-read display, inputs for multiple function switches and expression pedals, phantom power support, and the ability to send multiple PC and CC messages concurrently. You can also save the default state of instant-access switches on a per-preset basis. By the time you read this, an expansion module should be available to provide additional instant-access switches.

Tech 21 MIDI Mouse and MIDI Moose

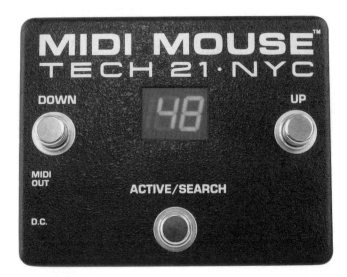

Fig. 6.21: Tech21 MIDI Mouse

Sometimes you don't need a lot of bells and whistles, but just something very simple that lets you select patches/presets on an audio looper, function switcher, or effects processor. Tech 21's MIDI Mouse and MIDI Moose do just that.

The MIDI Mouse and MIDI Moose have 128 presets apiece that send PC messages, with the only difference being the size and number of buttons. The Mouse utilizes simple Up/Down buttons to navigate, while the Moose gives you multiple preset buttons to step on within a single band. These can be powered by typical pedalboard power supplies, phantom power via a 5-pin DIN MIDI cable, or a 9V battery.

Fig. 6.22: Tech21
MIDI Moose

Also Consider

The number of choices for MIDI foot controllers is overwhelming. Many of the companies mentioned here have multiple products available, so if you don't need something as advanced as the models described above, there's a good chance that the company makes a scaled-down product that you can check out.

Other foot controllers worth considering include the CAE RS-5, Rocktron MIDI Mate, RJM MasterMind, G-Lab GSC-3, Mark L FX-25 Ace, Roland FC-300, and the Axess Electronics MFC5.

Because the MIDI spec hasn't changed in decades, there are some popular foot controllers, discontinued years ago, that are still widely used: the Lexicon MPX R1, ART X-15 Ultrafoot, DMC Ground Control, and the Roland FC-200.

CHAPTER 7

Audio Loopers and Amp Function Switchers

Audio Loopers

In the old days, pedals were either strung together in front of the amp or strung together in the effects loop of an amp. But why should your tone have to pass through multiple pedals when they aren't in use?

Today, we have *audio loopers* or *effects loopers* or *pedal loopers* that enable us to take all of our pedals and place them in their own discrete effects loops, hard bypassable, so when a pedal isn't in use, it's not even in the audio path. If you have lots of pedals, there is no easier way to clean up your signal chain than to put your pedals into their own loops.

Additionally, audio loopers enable you to end the famous pedal tap dance. By saving different configurations or snapshots of your pedalboard, a single button stomp can activate any combination of the audio loops, easily letting you go from your compressor and chorus pedals to your overdrive and delay pedals with a single stomp.

Configuring audio loopers is easy. You just take some short instrument cables from the In/Out jacks on your pedal and connect each of them to the desired loop number in the looper product, preserving the same order of effects as if you had laid them out in series on the floor: compressor, wah, chorus, delay, and so on.

All of your pedals get set to their On position, so you'll absolutely need an AC power source for them, and then the audio looper enables the use of each pedal by turning individual loops on and off. The beauty of this solution is that all pedal loopers have memory for multiple settings. Selecting your first preset might activate loops 1, 2, and 5; your next preset could activate loops 2, 3, and 6; your next preset could activate loops 1, 2, 4, and 7; and so on.

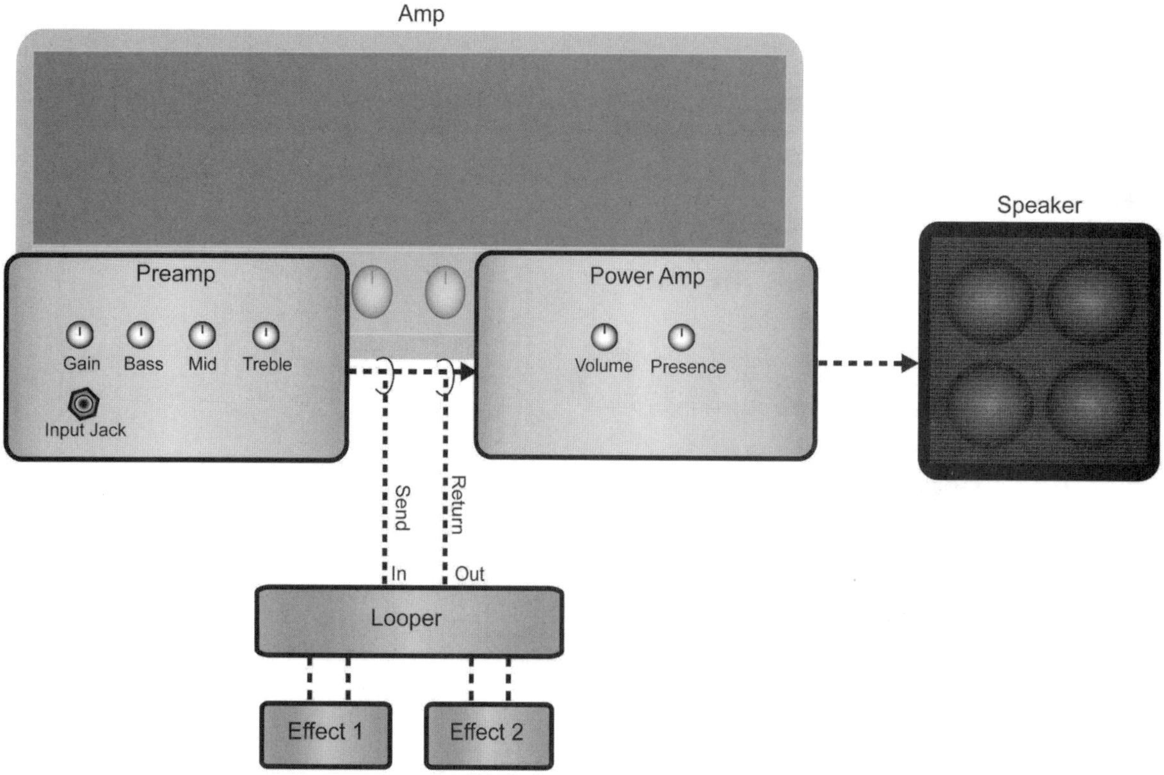

Fig. 7.1: Two pedals are shown connected to an audio looper in the effects loop of an amp.

As if this wasn't cool enough, I know some of you don't need all this memory stuff, but you'd love a solution that addresses one favorite pedal that you just can't get with true bypass. Never fear—check out Chapter 9 for a simple pedal that lets you add true bypass to any pedal.

Whether you're a pedalboard lover or a rack snob (and I call you that lovingly), there are audio loopers to meet your needs.

For the all-on-the-floor player, pedal loopers have multiple footswitches built in, and all of the pedal loops connect on the rear of the device. All are configurable with ease—there is no real programming to speak of.

But why step on your pedals if you don't have to? One of the great things about pedal loopers is that you can take all of your pedals off the floor and stick them on shelves in a rack, connect them to a rackmounted audio looper, and then use a MIDI foot controller to select your preset loops.

Separating Pre and Post Effects with a Looper

Using a pedal looper, it is possible to route some of your pedals to the front of your amp and other pedals to your effects loop. All this requires is (typically) the use of one of your loops as a break point in the signal chain. Your connections get routed like this:

➔ Put your front-of-amp pedals in the first few loops of your pedal looper.

➔ Connect the Send from the next open loop to the Guitar Input jack on your amp.

➔ Connect your amp's Effects Send to the input of the next loop in your looper.

➔ Connect your post-preamp effects to the next available loops in your looper.

➔ Connect the output or return of the final loop to your amp's Effects Return.

With this wiring scheme, turning off the loop at the break point bypasses your amp's effects loop entirely, and if you have function control switching over the loop, you might be able to hard-bypass it at the same time.

It should be noted that in loopers where some of the loops have insert points or independent loops not wired in series, you can typically use those loops to branch your effects pre or post without actually losing the use of the loop for one of your effects.

Amp Function Switchers

When you're building a rig that requires instant switching between your amp's many different functions, most pros ditch their amp's dedicated foot controller and use MIDI foot controllers to change the various settings on their amps. A *function switcher* is a piece of hardware that sits between the foot controller and the amp and provides an interface that the amp understands. Sometimes it's rackmounted; other times it's a box on the pedalboard.

An amp like the Mesa/Boogie Dual Rectifier Road King II has a huge foot controller with nine switches: four amp channels, Solo Boost, Effects Loop 1 On/Off, Effects Loop 2 On/Off, Reverb On/Off, and Mute. An amp switcher can give you MIDI control over virtually all of these settings so that a single foot controller can change your amp and effects settings at the same time.

Many function switchers and audio loopers can be configured to serve additional functions such as selecting between multiple guitars or amps. You'll find that there are numerous products on the market that combine both sets of features into a single product, since the basic electrical functionality for both audio loops and function switchers is similar. These combined products greatly simplify previously complex rig design.

Products of Interest: Many Overlapping Features

In the following sections, I have tried to organize products according to rack or pedalboard usage, looper or function switcher, but many products that provide audio loops also provide function switching as a secondary feature. Some products are switch-only. Be sure to explore each of the product categories that follow, since I may have categorized certain products based on their primary function just to keep things manageable. If you've only done your shopping at the big music chains, you'll be shocked to see just how many products exist to solve the looping and switching challenge . . . and I may have inadvertently omitted a few!

Floor-Based Audio Loopers

If you've got a pedalboard with multiple effect pedals, a floor-based looper can be placed directly on your pedalboard, typically in front of your pedals. Once you place your pedals in the loops of these products, you'll be stepping on the looper to select specific sounds.

Rocktron PatchMate Loop 8 Floor

Fig. 7.2: Rocktron PatchMate Loop 8 Floor

The PatchMate Loop 8 Floor is a sibling of the rackmounted PatchMate, and features eight mono audio loops that can be reconfigured for use in an amp channel–switching role. All loops feature true bypass, and the signal path can be either buffered or nonbuffered.

A MIDI interface enables the PatchMate Loop 8 to respond to MIDI control, useful if you decide to integrate it into a large rig with another foot controller. The PatchMate Loop 8 Floor has direct access to eight loop presets, but when controlled via MIDI, you gain access to up to 128 loop presets.

Cusack Pedal Board Tamer

Fig. 7.3: Cusack Pedal Board Tamer

The Pedal Board Tamer features nine true-bypassable loops, the last three of which are stereo loops, and it has memory for nine loop presets. It also adds a dedicated tuner output and a Tap Tempo switch that can control the tempo settings for up to three pedals (assuming they have an input for external Tap Tempo control). An All Off button gives you the ability to immediately disengage all active audio loops.

Carl Martin Combinator 2 and Octa-Switch

The Combinator 2 features eight audio loops, two of which feature stereo operation. With three banks of presets, it offers direct access to eighteen loop presets, and it also includes a dedicated tuner output, a master Mute feature, and three external switches for control of your amp. It also provides eight 9V power taps, so if you're using basic pedals, you don't even need an additional power supply on your pedalboard. Programming your loops is as simple as pressing a button to enable each loop and then hitting the Store button.

Fig. 7.4: Carl Martin Combinator 2

The less-costly Octa-Switch also features eight audio loops, but only one of them is a stereo loop. It has one bank of eight presets, and lacks the 9V power taps, Mute, and Tuner outputs of its big brother.

Fig. 7.5: Carl Martin Octa-Switch

Voodoo Lab Pedal Switcher and Commander

Taken on its own, the Pedal Switcher is the most simplistic of the pedal loopers, providing four mono loops without any memory for presets. However, it's designed to be paired with the Commander pedal, which adds memory for ten loop presets.

Multiple Pedal Switchers can be connected to the Commander via MIDI cables in a daisy-chain configuration—MIDI Out from the Commander to the In of the first Pedal Switcher, then from the MIDI Out of that Pedal Switcher to the MIDI In of the next one, and so on.

Fig. 7.6:
Voodoo
Lab Pedal
Switcher and
Commander

The GigRig Pro-14 and G2

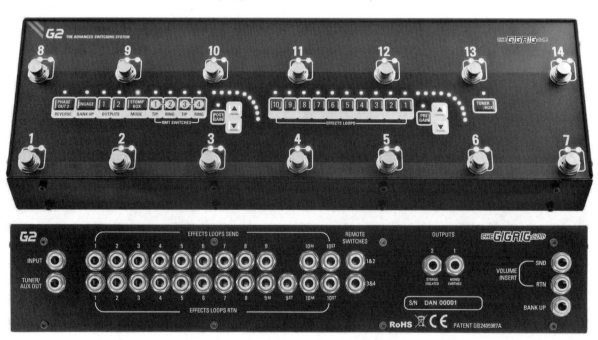

Fig. 7.7: TheGigRig G2 The new G2 marks the evolution of the Pro-14. Like the Pro-14, it has ten audio loops (two in stereo), and a pair of relay jacks enables switching up to four amp channels or other functions (like solo boost, etc.). It is a breeze to configure, and you can program gain levels for each loop to balance a wide range of effects and their levels, and the G2 has a volume pedal insert between loops 8 and 9. There are also two isolated outputs (one is phase reversible) so that you can switch sounds across two amps or one stereo rig.

The G2 borrows a page from the TC Electronic G-System's design: with the EXT option kit, you can split the rear interface from the foot controller and stick it in a rack for use with effects/pedals on a shelf, and then a single cable run from the rack to the foot controller provides power and MIDI control. When self-contained as in the photo above, the G2 can't run off of phantom power, but it will run off of most pedalboard power supplies (a 9V/350 mA wall wart is included).

Musicom Lab EFX Mk III+ Audio Controller

Another well-endowed pedal for pedalboard fans is the Musicom Lab EFX Mk III+. It features eight true-bypassable loops and four function switches for amp channel switching. There are two bypassable buffers, a volume pedal insert point between loops 4 and 5, a Mute switch, and a lot of great MIDI control.

Fig. 7.8: Musicom Lab EFX Mk III

The EFX Mk III+ transmits up to five PC messages and twelve CC messages, and it has sixty banks of presets, with four presets per bank.

Guitar Laboratory GSC-3 Guitar System Controller

The G Lab GSC-3 is a powerful solution for your pedalboard. It features six audio loops for pedals—and even provides six 9V DC outlets to power your pedals, Tuner output, true bypass loops and a buffered circuit, and two latching outputs for amp channel switching.

With MIDI capabilities, too (PC and CC messages, 10 banks of ten presets each), the GSC-3 puts full control of a compact rig in your pedalboard. Also check out the GSC-5 Guitar System Controller in Chapter 6. I filed it under MIDI foot controllers, but it offers many related capabilities.

Fig. 7.9: G Lab GSC-3

Decibel Eleven Pedal Palette and Switch Dr.

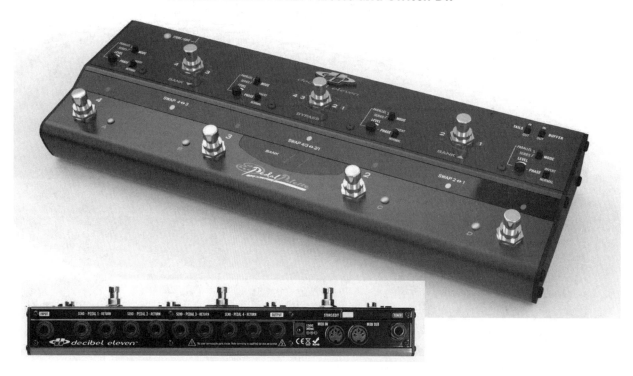

Fig. 7.10: Decibel 11
Pedal Palette

By now, you've read about numerous floor-based audio loopers, but none that are quite as sophisticated as the Decibel Eleven Pedal Palette, which takes the familiar audio looper paradigm and turns it on its head. Although the Pedal Palette only has four loops, it has one significant feature that distinguishes it from all others: you can swap the order of your pedals in the audio loops on the fly, and it enables you to run effects either in series or parallel with each other.

This clever audio routing capability earns the Pedal Palette a unique place in the floor-based looping category, as only the rack-based Sound Sculpture Switchblade (discussed later) offers this capability.

Additionally, you can route any or all of the loops in parallel, so the Pedal Palette is especially well suited to use with time-based effects like delays and reverbs.

Fig. 7.11: Decibel 11 Switch Dr.

The Switch Dr. has four audio loops arranged in a fixed order, but it adds two switching jacks for amp control and also adds a pair of MIDI jacks. The specs right now (the product is just coming to market as I'm writing this) call for up to three MIDI PC messages on three MIDI channels and eight CC messages across two MIDI channels, plus up to four MIDI Note-On messages, so you can use this controller to trigger sounds and samples on MIDI keyboards/samplers.

Also Consider

Other pro-caliber pedalboard audio loopers include the One Control Crocodile Tail Loop and the EC Pedals Custom Shop Super Switcher. The Crocodile Tail Loop has audio loops and MIDI functionality. The Super Switcher has five function switches for amp control independent of its audio loops, so you don't have to make an either/or decision as you do with some other loopers.

Rack-Based Audio Loopers

If you spend some time with a floor-based looper, you'll soon discover that unless you're a knob tweaker, there's really no need to have your pedals on the floor at all. Using a rackmounted audio looper, you can stash your pedals on shelves installed in a standard 19-inch rack and use a MIDI foot controller to select your effects. Many of your favorite touring pros rely on rack-based loopers so their pedals remain safely tucked away inside rugged equipment racks.

RJM Music Technology Effect Gizmo and Mini Effect Gizmo

Fig. 7.12: RJM Effect Gizmo

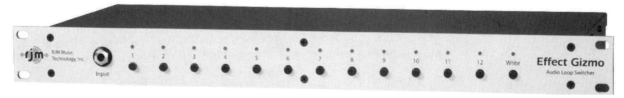

The Effect Gizmo features twelve audio loops, four of which are stereo. It can also be custom-ordered with all loops in stereo, and the last four loops can also be used for function switching such as changing channels on an amplifier. A buffer can be placed almost anywhere in the audio path—just not in between the four loops that are wired internally in series.

The Effect Gizmo, like many other RJM products, has the simplest programming interface of any gear you could ever hope to put in your rack, and with 256 memory locations, you can save a dizzying number of loop combinations. It also features a 7-pin DIN MIDI interface that provides phantom power to foot controllers.

The Mini Effect Gizmo is perfect for players who only have a handful of pedals but still need flexible routing options. The Mini has five loops, all wired in series, but you can sacrifice one loop to create a split point for pre and post effects.

Rocktron PatchMate Loop 8

Fig. 7.13: Rocktron PatchMate Loop 8

The PatchMate Loop 8 features eight mono loops, a buffered or nonbuffered input, and it can be used to control amp function switches. There is no internal connection between loops, though, so short jumper cables are used to route signals from one loop to another.

The PatchMate Loop 8 has 128 memory presets, and a 7-pin DIN MIDI connector provides phantom power. Additionally, the jacks can be configured for switching among multiple amplifiers.

Voodoo Lab GCX Audio Switcher

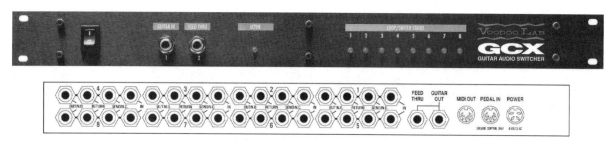

Fig. 7.14: Voodoo Lab GCX

The GCX Audio Switcher is extremely popular due to widespread availability—there's a chance you might actually find it in stock at a local music instrument retailer—and it has a great feature set. Functionally, it's very similar to the Rocktron PatchMate Loop 8, featuring eight completely independent mono true-bypass loops. As with the PatchMate, short jumper cables are required for connecting a signal from one loop to the next, and the loops can be used for amp function switching, too.

The GCX has buffered and nonbuffered inputs, and provides phantom power to foot controllers over a 5-pin DIN MIDI interface. The Voodoo

Lab Ground Control Pro foot controller features power over a 5-pin DIN too, making for an easy match. But since most MIDI foot controllers use a 7-pin DIN MIDI cable for phantom power, you'll probably need to connect to the GCX with a custom 5-pin to 7-pin DIN cable . . . like the one that Rocktron makes!

The GCX switches can be configured for amp function switching, and you can connect multiple preamps to it for switching among multiple amplifiers.

Rhodes Amplification B8 Blender

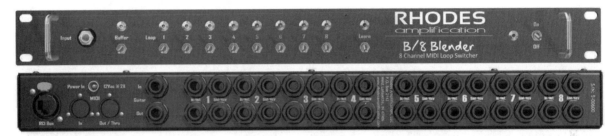

The Rhodes B8 is another eight-channel looper. From the prototype I looked at when writing this book, it has four connections per channel—In, Out, Send, and Receive, similar to the Voodoo Lab GCX and Rocktron PatchMate 8. But unlike those products, the jacks are auto-normalizing and do not require jumper cables for connecting the loops in series. With this wiring scheme, you get the best of both worlds—easy configuration for a series of effects as well as simple break points for placing some effects in front of your amp and others in the effects loop.

Fig. 7.15: Rhodes Amplification B8 Blender

This looper features a MIDI-bypassable buffer, and the front-panel guitar input automatically defeats the rear input, useful when you've got a wireless system patched into the back of the rig but you'd like to sit down and plug an instrument cable directly in.

The jacks can be used for amp switching, too, but due to the auto-normalizing loops, you'll have to use a shorted plug adapter to take advantage of this functionality. For additional details, visit the Rhodes Amplification website, as the product should be in production by the time you read this book.

Mark L Custom Guitar Electronics S-10 Audio Looper

Fig. 7.16: Mark L S-10

Mark L Custom Guitar Electronics makes fantastic infrastructure gear for your guitar rig, and the S-10 Audio Looper is one fine example of their work.

The S-10 provides ten audio loops, with the first six wired in series internally (for your front-of-amp effects). The next four loops are independent, so you can either connect them in series or use them all in parallel with the effects outputs running into a line mixer. Power to your foot controller is supplied via standard 7-pin DIN, or you can get a version of the S-10 that includes an XLR MIDI interface on the front panel for connection to Mark L MIDI foot controllers. There's also a dedicated tuner output as well as 9V and 12V output jacks to power some pedals.

Axess Electronics GRX4 Guitar Router/Switcher

Fig. 7.17: Axess Electronics GRX4

One of the most widely used pedal loopers in pro rigs would have to be the Axess GRX4. Straightforward in operation and compact in size, it features four audio loops, the first three wired in series. The fourth has insert points, and the unit can be operated in buffered or nonbuffered modes.

Rack-Based Function Switchers

If all you want to do is place your amp under MIDI control, there are a few products dedicated to the task. Some go in your rack, while others can simply be mounted behind your amp—just attach the switcher to the nice custom rack case you placed your head in.

RJM Music Technology Amp Gizmo and Mini Amp Gizmo

Fig. 7.18: RJM
Amp Gizmo

The Amp Gizmo provides eight function switches—enough to control most (if not all) of the footswitchable features on virtually every amp on the market—controllable from your favorite MIDI foot controller. It provides phantom power to foot controllers via a typical 7-pin DIN MIDI connection.

There are four stereo TRS jacks on the rear, and they support both momentary and latching switches. More elegant, though, is the RJM custom DIN connector that enables you to use RJM custom-made cables specific to your amp. Rather than running four insert or stereo cables from the Amp Gizmo to your amp (if your amp even supports these), get a custom cable for everything from Bogner to Diamond to Fuchs to Mesa/Boogie amps and more and just connect to your amp's standard footswitch jack.

Like all RJM products, programming the unit is really effortless. For example, step on preset #2 on your MIDI foot controller, select your amp's channel 3, enable the effects loop, and enable the reverb from the Amp Gizmo's front panel switches. Hold the Write button for a few seconds, and you're done! The next time you step on button #2 on your foot controller, you'll call up this setting.

The Mini Amp Gizmo is nearly identical, but is compact enough to install inside the back of your amplifier or place on a pedalboard—it can even operate from a 9V or 18V power supply. To save space, it requires use of a custom RJM cable for interfacing with your amp—there are no 1/4-inch switching jacks.

Another important design difference: if you want to control multiple amps, that's no problem with the Amp Gizmo since each jack is electrically isolated—no ground loop issues to deal with. The Mini Amp Gizmo, however, is only designed to control a single amp.

Fig. 7.19: RJM
Mini Amp Gizmo

If you have simpler amp switching needs, the compact Switch Gizmo (not pictured) works with any amplifier that uses standard ¼-inch switching jacks. It provides control of up to four switching functions and places them all directly under MIDI control.

Multi-Purpose Audio Loopers and Function Switchers

Because the electrical functioning of their jacks is so similar, many products on the market share dual roles as both function switchers and audio loopers. With multiple options in this product category, it has never been so easy to put a complex rig under MIDI control.

RJM Music Technology Rack Gizmo

Fig. 7.20: RJM Rack Gizmo

The RJM Music Technology Rack Gizmo packs a lot of features together into one rack space that are also available in smaller, single-purpose products in the line. The Rack Gizmo has eight true-bypass audio loops, the first four of which are grouped in series—no jumper cables required—while loops

5–8 are independent (and can be operated in stereo). There are buffered and non-buffered inputs, and a dedicated tuner output. The feature set is very similar to its predecessor, the RG-16; however, the buffer circuitry is upgraded, and the Rack Gizmo also includes Click Stopper technology that reduces the sound of switching some otherwise noisy effects.

When it's time for controlling your amp, the Rack Gizmo (and RG-16) has eight function switches, which can control amp channels, solo boost features, effects loop bypass, and a wide variety of features that modern amps contain. But rather than having a mess of ¼-inch cables between the Rack Gizmo and your amp like most products with amp control features, with RJM Music Technology you purchase custom cables that interface with your amp just like the original manufacturer's foot controller!

There is also a pair of mirrored switching outputs for control of a second identical amplifier, useful in a variety of multi-amp configurations. Finally, in addition to 7-pin DIN MIDI to supply phantom power to your foot controller, the Rack Gizmo features an XLR MIDI interface on its front panel for connectivity with RJM MIDI foot controllers.

Part of what makes RJM equipment highly praised (besides the audio quality and functional specs) is the extreme ease of use. You can program the operation of your loops and amp switching with zero knowledge of MIDI CC messages and using the simplest of foot controllers. Just step on a preset on your foot controller, push buttons on the face of the Rack Gizmo to activate loops and amp switches, and then hold the Write button for two seconds. Then, select your next preset on the foot controller, select the loops and switches you want, write the settings, and so on. It really is that easy to program.

Sound Sculpture Switchblade GL and Switchblade 8

Fig. 7.21: Sound Sculpture Switchblade GL

At first glance, the Switchblade units seem traditional enough: the Switchblade GL packs sixteen inputs and outputs into its single-rackspace chassis, while the Switchblade 8 has eight of each. Unlike many other audio loop products, the Switchblade makes it easy to assign any input directly to any number of outputs. In addition, the Switchblade GL has four switching jacks for controlling amps, and the Switchblade 8 has two. But if that's where you stopped reading, you wouldn't begin to appreciate the power stuffed inside this package.

One of the more unique features of the Switchblade line is that the order of the effects loops can be assigned on a preset-by-preset basis, and series/parallel effect placement is also assignable! Place your flanger in front of the delay and reverb on one song, then stick the delay in front on the next. Then run a few of your pedals parallel to each other. For the creative effect lover, this flexibility is pretty cool.

With its "combination network" you can customize running some effects in series and others in parallel, similar to some multi-effects processors, but with the flexibility of using all of your own unique effects devices.

The Switchblade is also configurable for bi-amping applications, running your signal to multiple preamps, and then supporting output to multiple amplifiers. It can be configured for mono or stereo operation (or multichannel sound if used in a studio or keyboard rig).

With the ability to respond to two MIDI CC messages assigned to control one or more connections simultaneously, the Switchblade GT can provide real-time control over things like crossfading effects, and with 125 presets (SB GT) and 75 presets (SB 8) accessible via MIDI, there's plenty of room to save your wildest effect creations.

With this advanced level of matrix routing, programming from the two-line display might seem intimidating to some players, despite a pretty intuitive interface. Fortunately, Sound Sculpture's Winblade software is a full-featured Windows-based software editor, particularly handy if you're creating a large number of different preset configurations.

Fig. 7.22: Sound Sculpture's Winblade software makes it easy to configure the extremely flexible signal routing within Switchblade products.

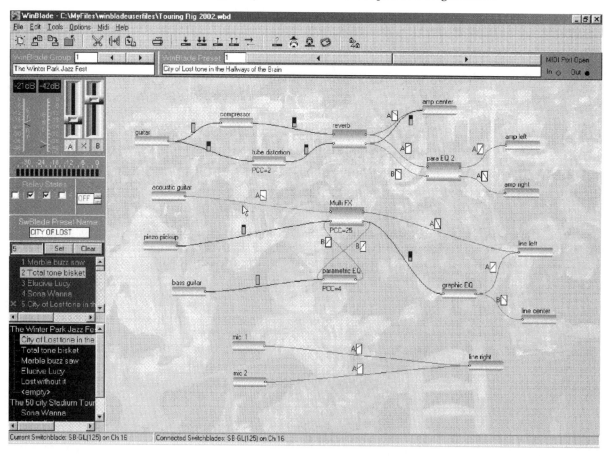

Mark L Custom Guitar Electronics LS 10/6
Audio Looper/Function Switcher

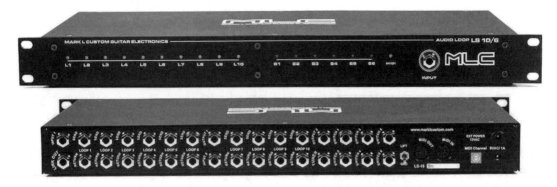

The new LS 10/6 is similar to products like the RJM Technologies Rack Gizmo, combining audio loops and dedicated amp function switching. First, you get ten audio loops wired in series, but with a break point after loop 6, so you can easily run some effects in front of your amp and others in the loop. Following the audio loops are six ¼-inch jacks for function switching of your amp or other devices as needed.

Fig. 7.23: Mark L S-10

As with other Mark L gear, 7-pin DIN MIDI is provided for phantom powering your MIDI foot controller, and some versions of the looper/switcher (like the Mark L B-16) have an XLR MIDI interface on the front for direct connection to Mark L MIDI foot controllers. The LS 10/6 also includes a dedicated tuner output as well as 9V and 12V output jacks to power some pedals.ed tuner output as well as 9V and 12V output jacks to power some pedals.

Guitar Laboratory MGC-6 MIDI Guitar Controller

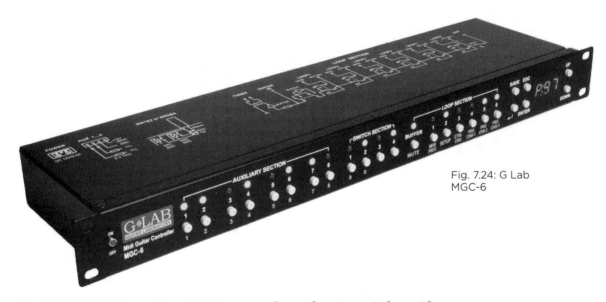

Fig. 7.24: G Lab MGC-6

The G Lab MGC-6 is another effects looper and amp-function switcher, with 100 user presets and direct MIDI control. Similar to the floor-based GSC-3, there are six true-bypassable audio loops, and two latching jacks for amp control. It can be expanded with other G-Lab products to provide amp A/B switching and additional audio loops.

Custom Audio Electronics

Think the other loopers and switchers here are too general-purpose and not me-specific enough? CAE can build you a custom switcher, looper, or combined product that offers the exact functionality you're looking for.

Floor-Based Function Switchers

There isn't much point to a pedal-based solution that only provides function switching, since the design of the unit automatically makes it well suited to audio loops. Be sure to check out the numerous floor-based loopers available, since most of those provide this capability.

Also check out the Mini Amp Gizmo from RJM Music Technology in the "Rack-Based Function Switchers" section. It's not really a rack item, nor is it specifically a pedalboard solution.

CHAPTER 8

Line Mixers: Helping Your Tone to Stay Dry and/or Parallel

ine mixers are primarily used to preserve the dry signal in your guitar rig so that effects processors with low-quality (or old) A/D converters, or effects pedals that color your unprocessed sound, won't destroy your guitar tone.

If your amp has a parallel effects loop, you've already got a mixer built right into your rig. After the preamp section of your amp, the signal gets split to your effects loop and to the power amp section of your amplifier (or to the main outs if you're using a dedicated rack preamp). A mix control lets you adjust how much dry signal goes straight to the output vs. being sent to your effects.

For amps with a series effects loop, an external line mixer can be used to create a parallel loop. This is useful when you want to guarantee that some portion of your tone remains 100 percent dry/unprocessed.

If you have a high-quality effects processor with 24-bit A/D converters, I don't expect you to hear any difference in your tone by running everything through your series loop and mixing wet/dry levels within the rack gear (once you've optimized your signal levels), but if you have an older 8-, 12-, or 16-bit effects unit, it can degrade the quality of your tone enough to really notice if your entire signal is run through the processor.

If you've placed pedals in your series effects loop, it's also quite possible that you have some tone suckers in there that will leave their mark on your sound, whether they are digital pedals or analog pedals that lack true bypass. Note that a pedal looper can keep unused pedals out of the signal chain, especially handy with pedals that lack true bypass.

Mixers in the Multi-Amp Rig

The series vs. parallel loop issue is only one reason for incorporating a mixer into your rig, and as soon as you "go big" with your rig, it becomes obvious where mixers can add some value. To start, it's very common to use a mixer when you'd like to share multiple effects devices between multiple amps.

In a multi-amp scenario, for example, you could run the Effects Send from multiple amps into a mixer so that two or more amps can share the same effects processors. Note that if you're using an audio looper, it is essentially a large mixer that provides some advanced control over signal routing. If you place one of these in your effects loop and connect multiple effects processors to it, you won't need a line mixer in this location within the rig.

Returning the signals from your multiple effects processors is a common location for line mixers in the signal path. In a wet/dry rig, you could simply send the output from a single multi-effects device to the input of a dedicated wet amp. But if you are running multiple effects processors in your loop, you'll need to send their outputs to a line mixer and then take the summed output from that mixer to the dedicated power amp for your wet rig. Most line mixers operate in stereo, too, so you can quite easily have multiple stereo effects units in your rig.

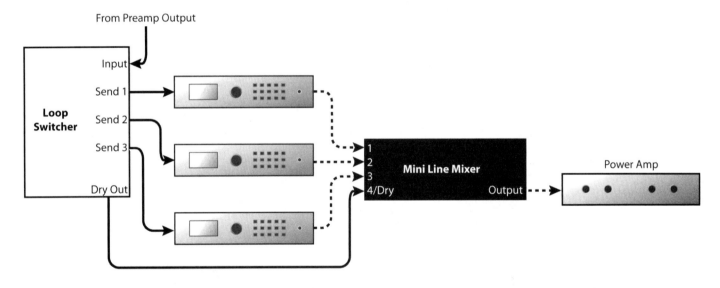

Fig. 8.1: In this example, courtesy of RJM Music Technology, an audio looper is used to send the guitar signal to multiple effects processors instead of a dedicated mixer. The stereo output from each processor goes into an RJM Mini Line Mixer, and a stereo output from the mixer goes to a dedicated power amp in a wet/dry/wet rig. Players with a stereo guitar rig could alternately send the outputs from the Mini Line Mixer right back to their preamp's stereo returns.

Mini Line Mixer Example Connection Diagram
Note: Stereo connections are denoted by dashed lines.

Some line mixers offer their own internal effects loops. You could run the Effects Send from one or more amps into a mixer and then place your effects in the loop of the mixer. To further complicate your rig, you could have multiple amps sending to the mixer and then place a looper in the mixer's effects loop.

As you can see, any way you might conceive of routing effects can be addressed with one or more mixers and audio loopers. It can be somewhat mind-boggling to explore the different ways to interconnect multiple amps and effects devices.

Don't Cut Me Off When I'm Busy Repeating Myself

Imagine a scenario where you've got a few effects processors running in an audio looper. You get to the guitar solo, step on your foot controller, and call up your soaring lead tone with a big delay from your TC Electronic D-Two and a cavernous reverb from your Eventide H8000. At the end of the solo, you step on your footswitch to go back to your crunch rhythm tone for the final chorus, and *bam!* Your reverb tail and delay repeats are gone!

To avoid this sonic fiasco, rather than having each effects processor return a signal to the audio loop in the looper, send the output from your effects into a line mixer, and have the output from the mixer go to your loop return. This way, when you change sounds on your foot controller to get back to your rhythm tone, disengaging the audio loops simply stops routing any of your signal into the delay and reverb units, but the repeats from the effects continue to occur until they are complete.

Products of Interest: Line Mixers

Note: All mixers listed as featuring stereo inputs or outputs also function in mono.

Custom Audio Electronics Dual/Stereo Mini Mixer

Fig. 8.2: CAE Dual/ Stereo Mini Mixer

Remember the scenario above where we needed one mixer to receive the Effects Send from multiple amps and another mixer to sum the outputs from multiple effects processors? The CAE Mini Mixer solves this challenge by providing two independent three-channel stereo mixers in one compact box.

RJM Music Technology Mini Line Mixer

Fig. 8.3: RJM Mini Line Mixer

The Mini Line Mixer is small enough to mount on your pedalboard, and features four stereo channels and a pair of stereo outputs. There's not much to say about this one: it's compact, can be used in all the ways described above, and like the other products worthy of mention in this book, it features outstanding audio quality and rugged construction.

Mark L Dual Stereo Line Mixer and Mini Line Mixer

Fig. 8.4: Mark L Dual Stereo Line Mixer

Mark L Custom Guitar Electronics offers two mixers for guitar rigs. The Dual Stereo Line Mixer is similar to the CAE Dual/Stereo Mini Mixer in that it offers two mixers in one box to handle complex setups with a single solution.

The first mixer offers five stereo inputs and the second mixer offers six stereo inputs. But the first mixer includes two sets of stereo outputs for cascaded parallel effect routing, running the first mixer's output to additional effects and then returning those effects to the first input of the second mixer.

Additionally, the Dual Stereo Line Mixer has a set of cabinet-simulated outputs.

The Mini Line Mixer is a simpler mixer available in two versions: one with two parallel loops and one with two loops wired in series. One typical use: Connect your amp's Effects Send to the input and then run two effects units in parallel with each other, then route the summed output from the mixer to your Effects Return.

CHAPTER 9

The Compact Rig: Modeling Amps & Profilers

I love tube amps. For guitar, there is no viable alternative that has the same presence and character of sound (or feel) as the real thing, at least to my ears. But . . . is there an alternative you can live with for those times you don't want to bring out the big rig? My tube-biased statement (pun intended) made sense five years ago, and thousands of guitar players still blindly stand by my assertion, but today, modeling technology has advanced so far that you can't honestly make that claim. In fact, many pros have turned to modeling rigs both for live use as well as for use in the recording studio.

Imagine being able to replace your amp and a rack full of effects (and a pedalboard filled with pedals) with a two- or four-space rack/gig bag and foot controller. Modeling technology has enabled players to build a "B" rig that is compact enough to carry onto an airplane for fly-in gigs and yet still sounds the same as their primary "A" rig. If you play with in-ear monitoring, you don't even need to bring a speaker cabinet to the gig!

Modeling amps and profilers offer some compelling advantages over the big rig. Besides the obvious savings in transportation costs when touring (or simply the gear-moving hassle), a modeling rig can provide numerous other advantages over a traditional guitar rig:

→Variety. Instead of having one or two amps with you for a show, your virtual rig can feature a nearly infinite variety of amps, effects, and speaker cabinets selectable on a song-by-song basis (or even preset-by-preset). A cover band guitarist can instantly switch from a Mesa/Boogie Dual Rectifier to a Vox AC30 to a Fender Twin at the touch of a footswitch.

→Reliability. There's no wear-and-tear like vacuum tubes experience. Your rig will sound consistent night after night without the risk of mechanical failure. There's never a need to re-tube or re-bias your modeled amp.

→Good sound at any volume level. Tube amps sound their best when pushed to a level that simply won't work in small clubs and definitely not in apartments or homes while the family and neighbors are sleeping.

→Cost. Your professional guitar rig may cost thousands of dollars between the amps, effects, line mixer, looper/switcher, custom rack case, cabling, line conditioner, etc. Even the most costly modeling rig may be less expensive overall.

Building a rig around a modeling solution has a number of variables to deal with, but overall the solution may be extremely straightforward depending on your needs. I'm going to explore multiple scenarios (and products, of course) that may provide you with the best solution if you're looking to head down this road for either your live rig or studio use, or both.

Modeling vs. Profiling

Modeling amps are virtual re-creations of analog amplifiers—both tube amps as well as solid-state amps. In short, electrical engineers/programmers analyze all of the internal components of an amp—from tubes to transistors to resisters to capacitors and more—and then, following the schematics for how the components are interconnected, they programmatically re-create the amplifier through software. Better-sounding amp models are, simply, better programmed than others are. The engineers have done a more accurate job of re-creating the analog product's design, from the amp's tone to how it responds when a hotter or weaker signal passes through the product to how both its tone and its response change when the amp's controls are set specific ways.

Profiling amps take a different approach to creating a virtual representation of your amplifier: they capture the sound of a specific amp as it is presently dialed in tone-wise on one specific channel at a time. Unlike the modeling approach, which re-creates entire amplifiers, profiling is more of a hybrid between audio sampling and the impulse response–capturing technology used by convolution reverb products. Rather than attempting to re-create an amp from the circuits on up, a series of test tones are run through the amplifier, and microphones connected to the profiling device capture the tones coming out of the speaker cabinet and record them as an audio profile.

The advantage of a profiling amp is that you can create profiles of your personal amps—with your tone settings—and then take your actual tone on the road in a compact "B" rig. Or you can rent a few of your favorite boutique amps, spend a day in the studio, and capture their sounds dialed in precisely the way you like them.

Effects can be modeled, too. As with amplifiers, programmers analyze the components of an effect/pedal and digitally re-create the product. Profilers haven't really tackled the effects category other than in the studio world of convolution reverbs, where they have captured the impulse response of thousands of locations. As a result, it's quite easy in the studio to place your amp virtually inside a famous cathedral, subway station, bathroom, or canyon.

Today, both modeling and profiling rigs can sound fantastic, and if you weren't looking at the rig, you would have no idea that virtual guitar rigs were being played. In some instances, even during an A/B comparison in the studio, players no longer discern the difference.

Popular Modeling Amps

Let's start out with the king of the modelers, the Axe-FX II. Artists are recording entire albums using nothing else, and even I have been duped, thinking I'm hearing some classic amp tone only to discover that I was listening to the Axe-FX on a recording.

Fig. 9.1: Fractal Audio Systems Axe-FX II

The Axe-FX II is both an amp modeler and effects processor, and the effects quality is so stunning that some artists use this device just for its studio-quality effects. Dream Theater's John Petrucci, for example, greatly simplified a few of his rigs by replacing multiple rack processors and shelves of pedals with the Axe-FX II to handle all of his guitar effects. But players have embraced the Axe-FX II not just for its tone, but also for its feel. It responds like you expect a real amp to respond.

When it comes to modeling, the Axe-FX II is loaded up with an extensive array of amp models, effect models, and speaker cabinet models. Plus, you can capture your own speaker cabinet impulse responses. An innovative Tone Match feature helps you nail the tone of a favorite recorded guitar sound, too, and a built-in USB audio interface provides a direct, digital connection to your computer for recording.

As a dedicated effects processor, the Axe-FX II can be set up with the four/five cable method so that some of its effects run in front of your amp and other effects run in your amp's series effects loop.

Fig. 9.2: Fractal
Audio Systems
Axe-Edit

The included Axe-Edit software makes it easy to create, load, and save custom sound presets, though you can control everything directly from the front panel of the unit. That said, the Axe-FX II is not the easiest modeler on which to dial in sounds, particularly from the front panel. It lacks dedicated knobs for adjusting commonly tweaked amp settings like EQ and Gain (though it has four assignable Quick Control knobs that can be assigned to desired settings). The unit's programmability is deep, and dedicated sound designers and tone-obsessed geeks will be in heaven. But less technical-minded players will find operation of the Axe-FX II a bit frustrating. It's not an instant-gratification device, but rather a professional (and sometimes complex) guitar amplifier tone-building tool. Indeed, with this great power does come great responsibility.

Fig. 9.3: Avid
Eleven Rack

The Avid Eleven Rack is many things: a modeler with amps, effects, cabinets, and microphones; a Pro Tools LE recording interface; and a re-amping device.

Operationally, Eleven Rack is simpler than the Axe-FX, and knobs below the display provide instant access for tweaking your amp sounds. If you've ever used amp modeling plug-ins within Pro Tools, then you'll be right at home with the software interface to Eleven Rack, which is the same as if you were just using the Eleven plug-ins without the dedicated hardware.

Eleven Rack hardware is advantageous over the plug-in-only approach, though, because of its guitar-optimized interface that adjusts to match the impedance of your guitar. And when tracking guitars into Pro Tools, Eleven Rack can automatically print your dry guitar sound to one track and effects to another mono or stereo track. Then, you can use the Eleven Rack as an output interface to re-amp the dry track through physical amps in the studio if desired.

Fig. 9.4: Line 6 Pod HD Pro X

The Line 6 Pod HD Pro X (and very similar predecessor, the Pod HD Pro) is a modeler and recording interface as well. The controls are intuitive, and I like that it has dedicated amplifier controls on the unit separate from four assignable controls that appear below the display. Unfortunately, the display remains pretty challenging to read, so programming your sounds is significantly easier to accomplish by using the free Line 6 Pod HD Pro Edit software.

Line 6 makes dedicated foot controllers for use with a variety of their amps, and connecting the FBV Shortboard Mk II (or other models) to the Pod HD Pro X gives you instant control over selecting presets and effects without having to learn a thing about MIDI foot controllers.

Fans of Line 6 effects are in for a treat because you'll find all of the company's effects inside—this is a far easier piece of gear to obtain than the older-but-classic rack effects such as Echo Pro, Mod Pro, and Filter Pro . . . and it also includes models of numerous pedals and effects from other companies. However, all of the presets come dialed in with amp modeling, so you'll have to do some basic reprogramming if you just want to use the device as a powerful effects processor.

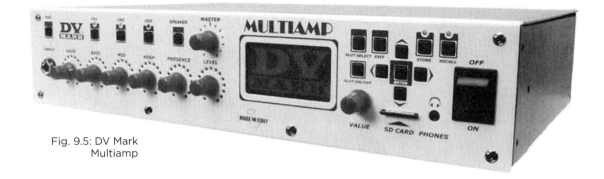

Fig. 9.5: DV Mark
Multiamp

The DV Mark Multiamp is a bit different from the other modelers in this gear roundup. It is configured like a traditional three-channel amplifier, but inside it's loaded up with models of amps, cabinets, and mics that you assign to each channel. (That said, there is memory to save hundreds of presets. Yes, that sounds confusing, but the layout is pretty straightforward in operation.)

The Multiamp goes one step further than the other modeling amps above, however, by also featuring a built-in power amp. While each of the preceding modeling amps requires an external power amp when used with speaker cabinets, the Multiamp features 150 watts into 8 ohms per channel (stereo), or it can be bridged for mono operation with ridiculous amounts of power (e.g., suitable for a bass rig).

Popular Profiling Amps

Fig. 9.6: Kemper
Profiling Amplifier
(KPA)

Equally as impressive as the Axe-FX II, Kemper is the sole purveyor of profiling technology thus far, and my MusicPlayers.com colleagues and I were blown away when it was first introduced to us. Right before our eyes, a product specialist profiled a Mesa/Boogie Road King II amp (which two of us owned), and then a minute later handed us the guitar and said, "Play." Proof positive, the tone and the feel were spot on. And after spending a considerable amount of time with the KPA in our studio, it continues to impress.

With the KPA, you create profiles of your amps by connecting a microphone to the back of the KPA and running an instrument cable from the KPA's output to the input jack of your amp. The KPA sends a series of tones through your amp/speaker cabinet (which you mike with the microphone of your choice), and it then builds the profile. If you have a four-channel amp (like my ENGL Powerball II), you would create profiles of all four channels if you wanted to take all of those sounds on the road. You're not limited, though, so you can then dial in a variety of additional tones in your amp and create profiles of those, too. And once a profile is created, you can even tweak both EQ and gain within a useful range (via big knobs directly below the display), so for live use, it's as easy to adjust as playing a real amp.

Part of what gives the KPA such great feel is that after you create a profile, you have controls to adjust/dial in tube amp sag, bias, and pick attack, so once you've got your sound, you can make the profile match the feel and response of your actual amp.

The Kemper Profiler comes loaded with numerous amp profiles to get you started, and it has a variety of useful effects built in as well. The KPA comes in two form factors: a lunchbox that looks like a '50s sci-fi ratio radio transmitter, and a three-space rack unit. Both versions are optionally available with a 600-watt digital power amp that changes nothing about the form factor, but enables you to easily power a pair of 4×12 cabinets.

Fig. 9.7: This compact rig features a power conditioner, Axe-FX Ultra modeler, and Matrix GT800FX power amp.

Building a Live Rig with a Modeling Front End

There are two different approaches to building a live rig around a modeler/profiler: pair it with a guitar-optimized power amp and guitar speaker cabinet(s), or pair it with a live sound/PA power amp and pair it with full-range PA speakers or monitors.

Since I crave real guitar tone all the time, I lean toward preferring the first approach. Running a modeling amp like the Kemper Profiler into an ENGL stereo tube power amp and then into an ENGL Pro 4×12 cabinet wired in stereo delivered truly incredible tone in my studio. Nobody who played the rig thought anything was compromised tone-wise versus an actual tube amp. This compact solution could easily cover any traditional rock/pop/alt/fusion gig. But the tube power amp is a bit heavy and delicate (tubes, you know). If only there were another option . . . and there is!

Britain's Matrix Amplification builds a line of solid-state power amps that are specifically voiced for use in modeling guitar rigs, whereas most solid-state power amps are full-range amps designed for use in PA systems. If you're done with carrying heavy tube amps around, a modeling solution paired with a Matrix power amp could be your ticket to heaven.

When we get to the output end of the signal chain, choice of speaker is another important consideration. If you're running your modeler/profiler into a guitar tube power amp or one of the Matrix amps, you'll want to connect the power amp to guitar speaker cabinets as appropriate for the rigs you make the most use of. So if you mostly use models of high-gain amps from the likes of Marshall/Mesa/ENGL/Soldano/Bogner, a 2×12 or 4×12 guitar speaker cabinet would be a logical choice.

If you want to rely fully on the modeled amp sound contained in your modeler/profiler, the other option is to use a solid-state power amp designed for studio or live PA use. There are numerous brands available to choose from, including QSC, Crown, Peavey, Mackie, Yamaha, Cerwin-Vega, and more. You won't hear much difference between them in your guitar rig, as the design goal is pretty similar among amps in this category: deliver lots of power as clean and flat in response as possible.

If you opt for a PA- or studio-worthy solid-state power amp, you're also going to want full-range speakers that deliver a flat frequency response (like studio monitors, for example). Atomic Amplifiers makes a line of speaker cabinets and floor wedge monitors optimized for studio-like flat frequency response, specifically for players of modeled amp rigs. Optionally, you could skip the power amp and get a set of powered PA speaker cabinets, too, but those are going to have a very hyped sound that will require spending some time adjusting the EQ in your modeled sounds. Atomic Amplifiers solves that problem by also offering their speaker cabinets/monitors with built-in power amps designed with the player in mind.

My Modeled Amp Sound Isn't Sounding Too Great on Stage

You won't be the first guitarist to build a great collection of presets in your modeler/profiler, pair it with a power amp and speaker cabinet, get to the gig, and then discover that the rig sounds horrible and doesn't even cut through the mix. I'm sure you won't be the last, either.

The sounds in your modeler are typically optimized for studio/recording use. There are so many variables in amps and speakers that I've talked about above, your modeler may in fact sound better in the studio and via its headphone jack than it does through an amp and guitar speaker cabinets. You may need to take some time to adjust EQ and properly dial in the overall tone of your sounds specifically as you hear them through your live rig. Don't wait until gig time to figure this out!

I would suggest saving two sets of each of your presets: one optimized for the studio/recording environment and a second set of presets optimized for your live rig. You may not be able to meet both needs with a single preset unless you're relying on in-ear monitoring to hear your guitar.

Modeling Speaker Technology

My chapter on rig infrastructure discusses dedicated speaker simulators and related modeling technology.

Solid-State Power Amps for Guitar Rigs

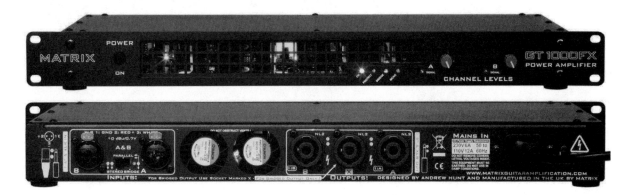

The GT1000FX 1u (typical street price: $800) is a single-space power amp designed specifically for guitar rigs, whether using a modeling front end or even a tube preamp. Inside, it's solid state, but optimized to deliver guitar amp feel and tone. My personal experience evaluating the previous generation Matrix GT800FX left me with a favorable impression. I would personally still pair a tube amp with a modeler, but the new GT1000FX may make me reconsider that decision.

Fig. 9.8: Matrix Amplification GT1000FX 1u

Another great use for the Matrix amps is with the "wet" speaker cabinets in a wet/dry/wet rig. For players not looking to have the wet amp color their effect tone significantly, these amps should definitely be considered. Matrix even makes a unique three-channel power amp for you to build simple wet/dry/wet rigs out of a modeling amp solution.

CHAPTER 10

Rig Infrastructure and Miscellaneous Goodies: Completing the System

There are so many components that go into building a pro guitar rig, someone could write an entire book about the subject and not even talk about anything that actually makes music! In this chapter we've got plenty of other essential yet nonmusical items you'll want to put in your rig, not to mention the actual rack cases.

I've also included a number of useful items that don't fit neatly into other categories in this book so you can get additional ideas for tools to enhance your rig.

Tuners

Most pros have rackmounted tuners installed in their rigs, often in addition to a compact tuner on the pedalboard. This enables guitar techs to plug guitars in for silent tuning even while the artist is on stage performing, and for players who use lots of rack gear, the rackmounted tuner provides a much larger display than you'll find on any pedals.

Rack tuners typically offer a wider array of features that are useful to players who rely on alternate tunings, as well as compensated tuning systems such as those found on guitars equipped with the Buzz Feiten Tuning System.

For years, the industry-standard tuner was the Korg DTR-1 Pro Tuner, followed by the DTR-2, 1000, and 2000. Who hasn't noticed that Cylon warrior eye onstage, a red dot moving back and forth in a rack behind some guitar player or bassist? Korg discontinued their rack tuners a few years ago, but just introduced a new Pitchblack Pro rack tuner for 2014. If your rig has a dedicated tuner output, then there's no real concern over the audio quality in a rack tuner, and you don't need premium cabling to hook it up, either.

Products of Interest

Peterson VS-R StroboRack Tuner

Fig. 10.1a: Peterson VS-R StroboRack Tuner

Today, the heavyweight champion title belongs to the Peterson VS-R StroboRack. Besides a traditional display of note values, it features Peterson's stroboscopic display, useful for both precise tuning and intonating a guitar.

Assuming you want to run your tuner in line with your audio signal, the expansion module for the tuner puts it in a league of its own. If your guitar has piezo outputs in addition to the magnetic pickups, both outputs can connect to the tuner, and then a built-in DI can send your piezo acoustic signal to a PA or other signal-processing gear.

The display can scroll custom messages—highly entertaining for those rock bands who want to send clever little messages to the groupies in the front row—and a built-in mic on the face of the unit is useful for tuning up acoustic guitars in the quiet of your studio. There's even a utility BNC gooseneck lamp socket on the rear in case you need additional lighting in the back of your rack.

Fig. 10.1b: The new Korg Pitchblack Pro tuner offers a low-cost alternative to the Peterseon VS-R, but with a simpler feature set.

Korg Pitchblack and TC Electronic PolyTune

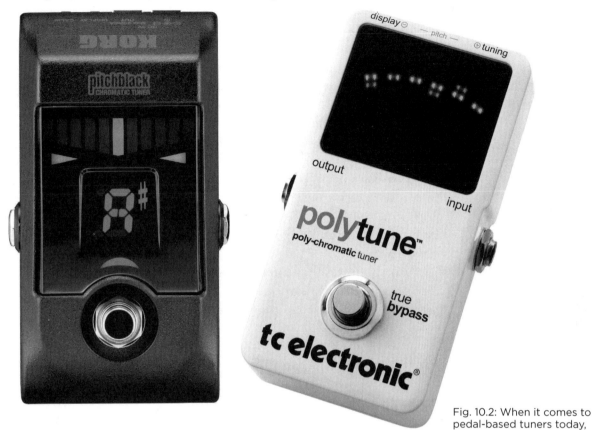

Fig. 10.2: When it comes to pedal-based tuners today, you'll see more of these units from Korg and TC Electronic than most other companies.

When it comes to tuners on a pedalboard, you certainly can't go wrong with a BOSS TU-3 Chromatic Tuner or TU-1000 Stage Tuner, but if you're looking to give your pedalboard a bit more panache, or if you insist on true bypass from your tuner, pros have been flocking to the Korg Pitchblack and TC Electronic PolyTune tuners.

Like the classic BOSS tuners, each of these pedals provides power to other select pedals, assuming that the proper specs are met, but each attracts different fans due to its unique properties. In the case of the no-frills Pitchblack, Korg crammed the useful display elements from its line of rack tuners into a true-bypass box that is smaller than even a typical BOSS pedal enclosure, making it useful on a small pedalboard, but with a very large and easy-to-read display.

TC Electronic revolutionized tuning in 2010 by introducing the world's first polyphonic instrument tuner. Strum all your strings, and the PolyTune shows you which strings are sharp or flat, or you can use it in single-string tuning mode, whereby it displays the note value you're tuning to with a virtual tuning needle above it. Yes, polyphonic tuning really works. The PolyTune Mini offers the same capabilities in an ultra-compact version of the pedal—nice if real estate on your pedalboard is at a premium.

Noise Suppression

Nobody likes noise from their guitar rig—even Strat and Tele players who insist upon their noisy vintage single-coil pickups. And nobody enjoys a noisy amp. Some high-gain shred machines can produce alarming levels of noise from their preamp circuits, and that's before you even begin to consider putting a distortion pedal in front of your amp.

Because of these very different locations in the signal path for generating noise, proper placement of a noise gate is critical, depending on your noise reduction objective. In the case of vintage pickups, you'll want to put a noise gate at the beginning of your signal chain, commonly before your volume pedal or compressor. But if you're trying to quiet a noisy high-gain amp, you'll want to place a noise gate in the amp's series effects loop (in a parallel loop, plenty of noise would go straight to the power amp without any benefit of noise reduction).

If you have rack gear and your rack preamp has a parallel loop, you get the best of both worlds: the benefit of the parallel loop for your effects, and being able to place the noise gate after the preamp's output on the way to the power amp.

Products of Interest

Rocktron HUSH Super C and HUSH Ultra

Fig. 10.3: Rocktron HUSH Ultra and Super C noise suppression units

Rocktron's latest generation of HUSH noise reduction products continues a decades-long legacy when it comes to quieting unruly guitar rigs. Good noise gates reduce unwanted noise without killing your guitar's tone or sustain, and these stereo (or mono) units will work beautifully with a full rack setup or in the effects loop of your savage head.

Both the Super C and HUSH Ultra incorporate the same noise reduction technology, with controls that let you tailor the noise reduction response to your specific needs, but the HUSH Ultra adds MIDI control! With this, you can selectively apply noise reduction only where needed, and with different levels and response characteristics.

The simpler Reaction HUSH pedal can be used on a pedalboard in front of your amp or in your loop, too.

ISP Decimator ProRackG and ProRackG Stereo Mod

If you're not using Rocktron, you're using ISP for noise reduction. And if you seek the flexibility of the HUSH Ultra but don't have a MIDI rig, be sure to consider the ProRackG.

Fig. 10.4: ISP Decimator ProRackG

With a slightly more involved connection scheme, your guitar signal runs first through the Decimator, and then the unit is also placed in your effects loop (it requires a series loop to function properly). By setting the controls for these two channels independently, one channel can take care of noise from your guitar while the other channel takes care of noise from your amp. Because your guitar signal is constantly running through the Decimator, the unit dynamically adjusts the noise reduction in your effects loop based on your actual playing.

For the pedalboard lovers among you, the Decimator G String is a pedal version of the ProRackG, and a simpler Decimator pedal is also available without the real-time signal analysis of the other models. Also, there is a custom stereo mod available for the ProRackG.

Piezo Pickups for Electric Guitars

Back in the '70s and '80s, having an acoustic guitar in your rig posed a special challenge: dealing with the transition from acoustic to electric guitar. For years, players used a special instrument stand to hold their acoustic guitar. The idea was that the player wore his electric guitar, but stood behind the acoustic guitar stand and reached up to play the immobilized instrument during acoustic passages. When the time was right, the player would just switch to playing his electric guitar.

These days, it's very common to get an electric guitar with a piezo acoustic element installed under the string saddles, and this combination of magnetic and piezo pickups opens up a whole new world of musical opportunities.

Piezo-equipped guitars have either dual mono output jacks or a stereo jack, and a pickup selector switch on the guitar lets the player choose between magnetic tone only (your traditional electric guitar tone), piezo acoustic tone only, or both sounds at the same time.

Typically, the magnetic pickup output from your guitar runs to your guitar rig and the piezo acoustic output runs to the PA system or a dedicated acoustic guitar amp. Layering an acoustic guitar part on top of your heavy electric guitar tone brings a classic studio recording technique to your live performance, and you don't have to play in a Led Zeppelin tribute band to appreciate this sound.

The other obvious advantage of the acoustic-in-my-electric tone is the ability to instantly switch from acoustic song sections to heavy sections.

The sound of a piezo-equipped electric guitar can easily convince music listeners that they are hearing a true acoustic guitar, and there is no contest between piezo acoustic tone and the best clean tone from a traditional solidbody guitar's magnetic pickup. Once you play a guitar with the acoustic output running through a clean amp or PA while you jam on your electric tone, it's hard to go back to a guitar without this fantastic option.

I can't stress enough the need for a true acoustic guitar amp or a channel in your PA system for your piezo acoustic tone. It just won't sound authentic if you play it through your tube amp on a clean channel. It needs to be routed to a full-range speaker system like your PA system for you to really hear and appreciate the difference in sound.

On some guitars, the piezo acoustic sound straight out of the instrument is a bit lacking. It sounds "just okay" until you hear what a difference the right processing can make, and it's this processing that transforms the sound of some piezo-equipped guitars into something that really sounds like an acoustic guitar.

Products made for enhancing the sound of amplified acoustic guitars work incredibly well on piezo-equipped electric guitars. Once you get your hands on one of these guitars, be sure to place one of the following items in between the guitar and the PA system to really take your acoustic tone to the next level.

Products of Interest: Direct Boxes for Piezo-Equipped Electric Guitars

L.R. Baggs Para Acoustic DI and Venue DI

Fig. 10.5: L.R. Baggs Para Acoustic DI and Venue DI

Plug into one of these DIs and your piezo tone will be transformed even before you start tweaking the fine parametric EQs. Both units have an effects loop, too, so you can add some dedicated effects to your acoustic tone.

The Venue DI takes things further by incorporating a tuner and a volume boost, footswitch controllable, but the extra features sacrifice the Para DI's ability to be powered from your PA system's phantom power.

Fishman Aura Spectrum DI and Aura 16

Fig. 10.6: Fishman
Aura 16

The Fishman Aura DIs were created to apply acoustic guitar modeling to acoustic guitars with built-in pickups in order to restore the natural sound of those guitars miked up in a recording studio. If you're playing a spruce-topped dreadnaught acoustic with a rosewood back, select the image of a similar model guitar, and then the Aura mixes that modeling with your acoustic's onboard electronics to create a much better acoustic tone.

Imagine the surprise of the engineers at Fishman when players like Alex Lifeson and John Petrucci started using these products with their piezo-equipped solidbody electric guitars!

The Aura 16 is all you really need if you plan to experiment with your electric guitar. The Spectrum DI adds memory for additional acoustic models, an onboard tuner, and a compressor. In both cases, new images can be downloaded from the Fishman website and loaded into the pedals via a USB interface.

Radial Engineering ToneBone PZ-Select

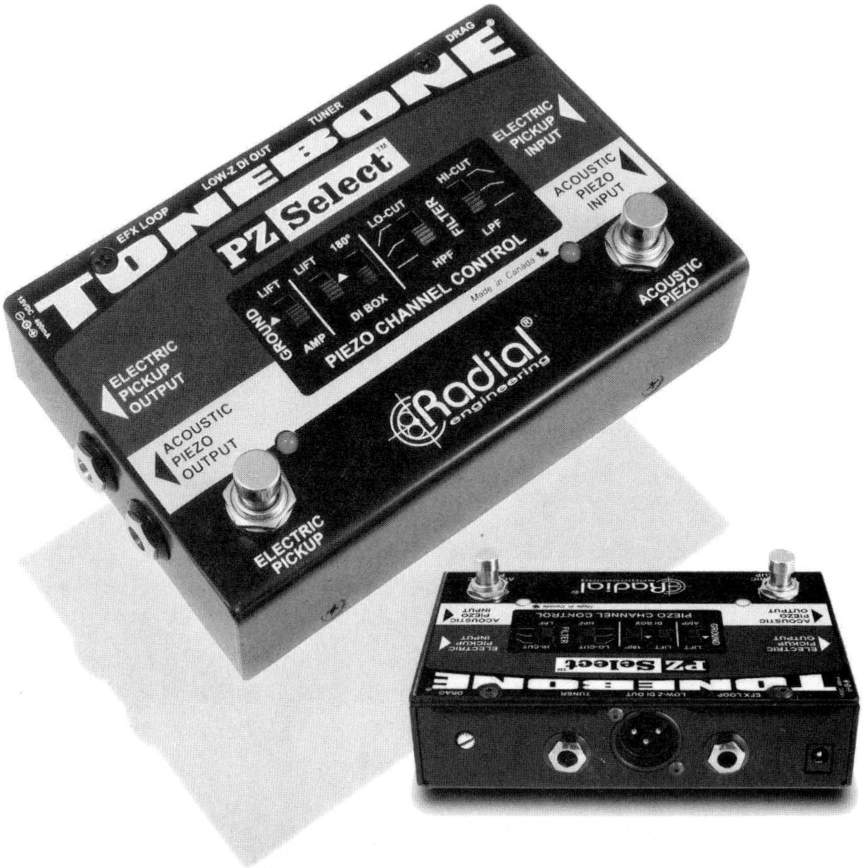

Fig. 10.7: Radial ToneBone

I Love Radial. They are the Swiss Army of studio and rig infrastructure products, and if there's something you need to accomplish but can't find a product that does it, odds are good that they make a product to meet your needs.

The PZ-Select is one such fantastic item: a piezo and magnetic pickup selector and direct box built into one! If you find it difficult to switch between the magnetic and piezo acoustic output of your guitar quickly because the switch is buried in the cluster of knobs and switches on your guitar, then the PZ-Select is an answer to your prayers. It enables you to switch the outputs on your guitar instantly via a footswitch!

To use the PZ-Select, you connect either a stereo/TRS cable or a pair of mono instrument cables from your guitar to the PZ-Select, and then cables run out of the ToneBone device into both your guitar amp and your acoustic amp or PA system.

There are numerous controls that enable you to dial in pickup resistance, a hi-cut filter, and more. But keep in mind that with this setup, your piezo output will be active all of the time, so you'll burn through more 9V batteries.

Products of Interest: Electric Guitars with Piezo-Acoustic Outputs

If you're shopping for a piezo-equipped solidbody electric guitar, there are numerous brands to consider. Two of the most popular manufacturers include Parker Guitars and Music Man Guitars. The Parker Fly was the first iconic electric guitar to catapult this option to popularity, and almost every guitar in the Parker product line features piezo acoustic output in addition to the magnetic pickups.

Fig. 10.8: The Parker DF624 has softer lines than the original Parker Fly and offers equally effortless playability and great features.

While Parker guitars are amazing instruments, the Music Man John Petrucci signature models top all guitars on the market for the logic of their piezo implementation. On many guitars—including most Parker Fly models, the switch for magnetic/piezo/both pickup selection is located within the cluster of knobs and pickup selectors for the electric guitar controls. But on the Petrucci guitars, the selection control is placed by itself on the upper horn of the guitar, making it easy to hit for instant switching from acoustic to electric tones.

Fig. 10.9: The Music Man John Petrucci signature models place selection of the piezo output by itself on the guitar's upper horn for instant access in mid-song.

Many piezo-equipped electric guitars feature a stereo output jack, and from there you run a stereo cable to a breakout box, or you get a special cable wired for stereo at one end and dual mono cables at the other end. With the Petrucci guitars, there are dual mono jacks on the guitar for two cables (or connecting two wireless transmitters). But if you prefer, you can connect a stereo cable to the first jack and run that as described above.

If you're a fan of guitars with more heft than Parker Fly and Music Man Petrucci guitars, the Gibson Les Paul Alex Lifeson is one you'll want to check out. Also consider Brian Moore Guitars, custom guitar options from Carvin, and other Music Man models with piezo options.

Fig. 10.10: Many custom guitars from Carvin are available with the Graph Tech Ghost system installed, with or without MIDI, and with a variety of bridge styles.

Products of Interest: Piezo Upgrades for Your Current Guitar

The Graph Tech Guitar Systems ghost Pickup System relies upon new string saddles that include piezo acoustic elements. If your guitar has a Strat- or Tele-style bridge, a Floyd Rose Original or Licensed bridge, or a Wilkinson tremolo (among others), there's a great chance that Graph Tech has parts available to retrofit your guitar. Or you can purchase completely assembled bridge replacements.

In addition to adding acoustic guitar tones to your solidbody electric, the ghost system can optionally add a fast-tracking MIDI interface to your guitar that is fully compatible with Roland's standard 13-pin system and subsequently every guitar synth on the market.

Speaker Emulations and Power Attenuation

Miking a speaker cabinet is one variable that many pros like to eliminate from their live rigs, instead relying on *speaker emulation* or *cabinet simulation* technology to deliver a miked sound to the front-of-house engineer.

Pros including Alex Lifeson, Keith Richards, Warren Cucurollo, and Eddie Van Halen have all made use of simulators built by Palmer Musical Instruments. These devices typically run in-line between your amp's speaker output and your speaker cabinet, allowing you to retain your cabinets for stage volume, not to mention their striking good looks. But if you could care less about the cabinets—in-ear monitor users have little need for them anymore—you'll need to purchase simulators that have built-in load boxes that match the specific wattage and ohm ratings of your amplifier's output.

For recording guitars, the classic cabinet simulators are useful tools when you're confined to quiet spaces and want to use your favorite amp, but some exciting new products have taken cabinet simulation to an entirely new level through the use of modeling technology.

Attenuators are other useful tools for the serious guitarist. They enable you to run your amplifier at very high output settings but with manageable volume levels. Whether you're trying to cop the sound of a classic recording by playing a non-master-volume Marshall amp at "10," or you just love good power tube saturation but can't deal with the obscene stage volume, these devices can be a great addition to your rig. Be sure that the attenuator matches the appropriate wattage and ohm rating of your speaker output or you'll do some real damage to your favorite amp.

Products of Interest: Speaker Simulation

Palmer PGA-05 Advanced Direct Injection for Guitar—Stereo

Rack lovers rejoice! The dual-channel PGA-05 works great with a stereo rig, and a line/speaker-level input switch enables you to use it directly with a guitar preamp. However, there is no load box built into this model, so you must connect a speaker cabinet.

Fig. 10.11: Palmer PGA-05

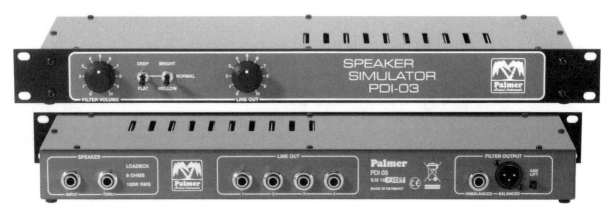

The PGA-04 ADIG-LB is a single-speaker cabinet solution with a built-in load box, so you don't need to bring a cabinet on the road with you. It is a newer version of the popular PGA-03, which has been upgraded with more extensive control over the sound of the simulated cabinet output. The PGA-03 has been reissued, though, due to overwhelming popularity. Some players love to stick with what they know.

Fig. 10.12: Palmer PGA-03

Two Notes Audio Engineering Torpedo VB-101 and VM-202

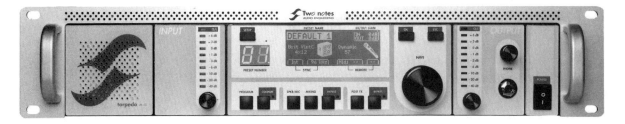

Fig. 10.13: Two Notes Torpedo VB-101

While the Palmer devices are widely used onstage, expect to see many pros switching to the Torpedo products. These technology marvels are true cabinet and microphone simulators built around convolution technology, a fancy studio technique used in capturing and modeling acoustic spaces.

The VB-101 connects to your amp's speaker output, passing or not passing the signal along to a cabinet. Inside the box, you have a choice of modeled speaker cabinets, microphones, and microphone placements. If you've got a studio of your own, Two Notes provides software to capture your own impulse responses from your actual speaker cabinets and load them into the VB-101.

Fig. 10.14: Two Notes Torpedo VM-202

The VM-202 is a two-channel box (stereo rig lovers rejoice!), but rather than capturing your amp's output, it captures a line-level output from your preamp and delivers power amp modeling in addition to the speaker modeling technology found in the VB-101. With a choice of tubes (EL-34, 6L6, etc.) and amp topology (Class A, AB, etc.), this is another versatile tool, though a bit more likely to be used in the studio.

With the capabilities found in these two units, they are incredible tools for the studio. But sadly, most guitarists can't afford to use these in their live rigs. If only there were a less costly option . . .

Two Notes Audio Engineering Torpedo Live

The Torpedo Live gets some lengthy coverage here because it is, quite frankly, the speaker simulator you want to have in your rig. I have it in mine, and my friends now have it in theirs. It's the game changer in the speaker simulation product category.

    As a load box, the VB-101's baby brother lets you crank your amp quietly. You connect the speaker output from your amp (up to 100 watts into 8 ohms) to the Torpedo Live's input. Next, you connect an audio cable from the Torpedo Live's balanced or unbalanced output to your preamp (for recording) or your mixing board (for live sound) . . . or just plug in a set of headphones. Then, rock out. If you'd like to hear your amp out loud, simply connect your speaker cabinet to the speaker output jack and the signal passes through. Or just play and record while the kids are sleeping.

    In the Torpedo Live, you select the speaker cabinet of your choice from a healthy selection of popular modeled cabinets, all built from actual impulse responses captured through the real cabinets, and then you select a virtual microphone from a list containing all of the popular ones (for guitar), including models of the Shure SM57, Royer R121 Ribbon, Sennheiser MD421, Neumann U87, and more. Finally, you move the mic position on or off axis and adjust its distance from the speaker cabinet (front or back).

Fig. 10.15: TwoNotesTorpedo

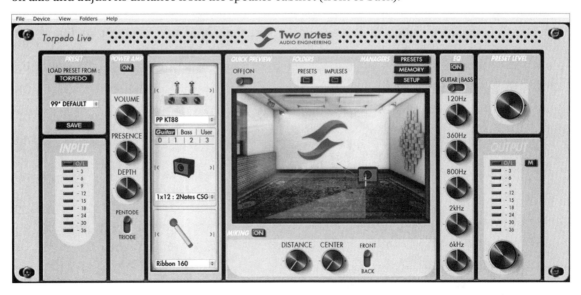

Fig. 10.16: TwoNotes Torpedo Remote

The front-panel interface on the Torpedo Live is very easy to use, but the free Torpedo Remote software makes configuring your speaker/mic modeling a total breeze.

The sound quality is stunning. While reviewing the Torpedo Live for MusicPlayers.com, our mission ended up being to see if we could mike our cabinets in the studio with the same mics that were modeled and match the quality of the sound from the simulated output. I think we came pretty close.

You can put the Torpedo Live in your rig for under $1,000. Need I say more? Okay, just a little bit. First, it also has power amp modeling, so you can take the output from your Axe-FX modeler or Triaxis tube preamp and pair it with some great-sounding virtual tube power. But if you want to put two virtual mics on your modeled speaker cabinet, you'll need to spring for the VB-101, which also supports up to 120-watt amps. But that device is twice the size and twice the price.

Products of Interest: Power Attenuators

THD Hot Plate Attenuator

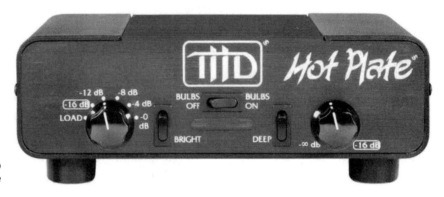

Fig. 10.17: THD Hot Plate

By far the most popular attenuators on the planet must be the THD Hot Plate series. Although available in a range of hot colors, you must use the model that is specific to the power and speaker ratings of your intended amplifier.

Each Hot Plate can attenuate the output volume from 0–16 dB. Vintage Marshall and Fender amp owners rejoice, as you can now crank those classics *and* be in the same room with them! Furthermore, the Hot Plate can provide a resistive load, so you can operate your amp without a speaker cabinet and take the Hot Plate's Line Out direct to your recording studio interface or your PA system. Note that the line output is not the same thing as a good cabinet simulation, but if you have *that* in some other gear or via a studio plug-in, the line out can prove quite useful.

Two Notes Audio Engineering Torpedo LB-202 Load Box

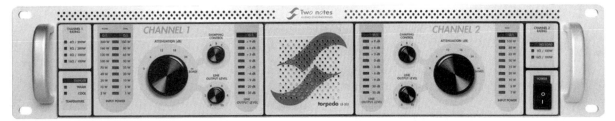

The Torpedo LB-202 is a two-channel attenuator capable of operating with speaker outputs of 4, 8, and 16 ohms in a single device. Perfect for pairing with a high-powered tube stereo power amp or two amps in a wet/dry rig, it can also be paired with the Torpedo VM-202 dual speaker simulator for both studio and live purposes.

Fig. 10.18: Two Notes Torpedo LB-202

Rivera RockCrusher Power Attenuator and Load Box

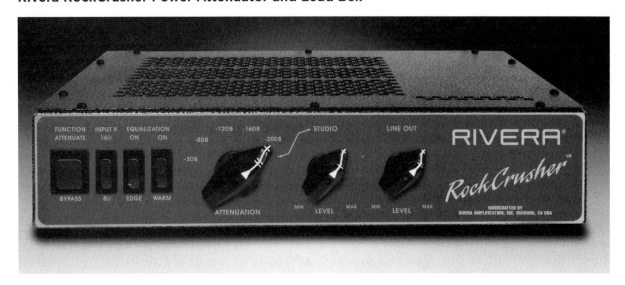

The RockCrusher works with 8- and 16-ohm speaker outputs and adds a few preset EQ switches to shape the tone if desired. The unit may be bypassed at the flip of a switch, and a Studio setting optimizes your tone for use at apartment volume levels.

Fig. 10.19: Rivera RockCrusher

Power Conditioning

Whether you're touring the world, playing the local club scene, or playing the nice-toys-in-my-bedroom scene, protecting your delicate guitar amplifiers and effects, and maximizing your tone, is essential. Power fluctuates constantly from the grid to the venue (this includes your home), and in a perfect world, you would have precisely 120V @ 15 amps (in the United States) coming out of the electrical socket and into your gear, since this is what it was optimized to work with.

Brownouts are obvious dips in delivered power, and we all know that lightning strikes can cause far larger power surges than your gear is prepared to handle. But the routine spikes and dips that happen daily are what really

117

add wear and tear to your power supplies and electrical components.

As if a regulated flow of power wasn't enough to worry about, the *quality* of that power can also affect your guitar tone. Unless you've got the only hut with electricity on a desert island with its own power plant, it's quite likely that there is a significant amount of electrical noise in your incoming power, too. Whether it's from electrical appliances, air-conditioning units, electronic devices like computers and televisions, or fluorescent lights, all of these items and more add low-frequency noise to the incoming power . . . and your gear passes that noise on to the speakers, even if it's at a level you don't notice!

Although it's not immediately apparent to your ears, unfiltered noise in the incoming electricity can make the low-end frequencies in your tone lose clarity. In fact, if I were writing a book about building video-editing suites, right about now I would be talking about how this electrical noise can actually be seen in some video transmissions.

Where is this conversation going? Well, the obvious first point is that if you're just using a $10 surge suppressor/power strip from Home Depot to protect your guitar rig, you really aren't doing much. The *only* thing you're doing is protecting against a power spike—or are you? How long have you been using that power strip? Those devices are built with components designed to handle one big spike; then their components are toast, and it's time for a new surge protector. However, the constant fluctuations in power at your home and at your gigs wear down the components inside those power strips. When the big spike hits, your surge protector may not provide the same level of protection—if any—that it was originally designed to handle.

There are numerous devices engineered to provide a regulated flow of current, filter out the noise that degrades your audio signals, and protect against significant power spikes without destroying the actual protection equipment. And although you may only think about lightning delivering that really bad power spike, touring professionals face a far more frequent concern over proper voltage, both domestically as well as internationally.

A story all too familiar with touring techs is that someone accidentally plugs a guitar rig into a service power line at a concert venue that is carrying far more current than expected, and blows up all the gear. How can this happen? Take a product built for use in the United States with a fixed power supply, go to Europe, get an adapter for the plug on your power conditioner so that it can fit into the different-shaped sockets, but don't do anything to step the current down from 240V to 120V. Sit back and enjoy the fireworks display.

Furman is the undisputed leader in power protection in pro music rigs, and you'll find its gear in more pro rigs than any other company's products. But stay away from entry-level units like the company's Merit series, as they lack too many important features.

Am I the only musician who ever wondered whether their surge protectors were actually providing protection when switched off? We all use our line conditioners and power strips as master on/off switches, but if they're off, what happens when lightning strikes? Rest easy, friends. If your house doesn't burn down and a surge runs through the power lines to your gear, in most cases, the surge protection is one element of nearly all power products that remains functional when off. Furman's Christos Desalernos explains, "Most simple strips only disconnect the hot line with the power switch. The surge suppression is still in the circuit, and will protect if a surge comes down the neutral [line] or arcs over the hot terminals inside the switch. If there is an overvoltage circuit, then that will be defeated if the power switch is off."

Products of Interest

Furman Classic Series and Power Factor Power Conditioners

Fig. 10.20: Furman power conditioners

For the budget-conscious player, I love the PL-Plus DMC and PL-Plus C. They feature surge protection, noise filtering, and Furman's EVS extreme voltage protection. If there's a problem with the facility wiring, a steady flow of too much power could kill your gear, and unlike surge protection, this is a constant stream of too much power. If more than 137V shows up on the AC line, a relay immediately shuts down the unit.

These units only differ in their display of the incoming voltage range: the DMC has a digital readout showing the exact voltage, whereas the C has a typical voltage meter. Either way, if you've never had a voltage display on your gear, you'll find it particularly satisfying to own this gear once you see how much your supposedly good studio wiring fluctuates.

Stepping up to the P-1800 PF R puts you in the major leagues. You gain Furman's Power Factor Technology, which ensures that power is delivered to your amp with a constant level of resistance on the line. At low resistance, power flows rapidly into your amp, and your tone is what you expect. But in a venue where there is high resistance on the line—caused by many factors, including distance from the power pole—current flows at a slower rate to your amp, resulting in your amp lacking the tone definition you expect to hear.

A 45-amp current reserve in the P-1800 makes sure that your amp receives power at a consistent and fast rate. This unit also adds an additional layer of noise filtering beyond the PL-Plus models. If you play the club circuit and find your amp's response seems to change in some hard-to-quantify manner from venue to venue, the quality of the power could easily contribute to your problems, and stepping up to a device like the P-1800 might make a significant difference to your rig.

Great power doesn't stop there, however. The P-1800 AR adds RMS voltage regulation. If you want a constant 120V without variance, you'll get that here. But since it lacks some of the features in the PF R, it's common for pros to have both units in their rig, with one unit daisy-chained off the other.

If a world tour is in the offing, Furman has larger systems that can provide a regulated 120V regardless of what the voltage standard is in the country you're playing in, but be warned. Units like the AR-Pro will add fifty pounds to your rack.

Also Consider

The Monster Pro Power for Musicians series, the Juice Goose RM 115, and the Samson PowerBrite PB15 Pro.

Wireless Systems

I've been using wireless systems for guitar for many years with great success both onstage and in the recording studio. Yes, I even ditch the wire in the recording studio! Given that today's pro-level wireless systems sound just as good as a wired tone, it surprises me that some pros still play live tethered to an instrument cable. In fact, if you talk to some of the custom rig builders featured in this book, they'll try to steer you away from wireless systems, too.

An instrument cable is going to work all of the time without worrying about interference from other broadcast sources, so the cable does have that advantage. And you don't need to keep a set of freshly charged batteries handy. But that's where the advantages end.

The past few years have seen an explosion in the availability of both high-quality and low-cost digital wireless systems. These products sound so good that there just isn't any reason to consider an analog wireless system.

Analog wireless systems sound great sometimes—don't get me wrong—but they have some serious limitations. First, they rely on a process called companding of the audio signal. In the transmitter, the signal is compressed before transmission, and then it is expanded at the receiver. The reason is simply that the instrument signal has a greater frequency range than the transmission technology can actually transmit, and this is why players with critical ears observe that their wireless tone sounds slightly compressed. In truth, it has been compressed. And the limited frequency bandwidth is why analog systems never sounded as good on bass as a wired tone does.

Digital wireless systems eliminate the companding issue entirely. Boasting full frequency range transmission, these systems easily cover 10 Hz to 20 kHz and have an analog-to-digital converter in the transmitter. These are spec'd well for your critical listening pleasure: 24-bit, 96k. From there, it's a bunch of zeros and ones sent through the air to the receiver, where your tone is reassembled and sounding fantastic.

Even in the studio, it would take a very critical A/B test to hear a difference in tone, and it would probably require a full-bandwidth tone, like a clean, just barely breaking-up sound, played in many styles and in many octaves, to find the audible differences. Throw your performance into the mix with other players and you will never notice a difference in sound or feel. In "typical" comparisons (I've reviewed numerous wireless systems), serious players just don't hear a difference these days. So if you want to run around on stage like the rock star you undoubtedly are, go for it. And bass players are welcome, too! Don't forget to send me a ticket to the show.

Pros

→ Complete flexibility to run around onstage like the rock star you are.

→ Ability to stand near the front-of-house engineer during soundcheck to make sure he's nailed your tone.

→ Ability to stand in the recording studio control room during tracking while your way-too-loud amp is isolated in another room. There are wired solutions for this recording scenario, but wireless makes it effortless.

→ The signal from your guitar is buffered, ensuring that a strong signal hits your amp or effects pedals.

→ No ground loop issues between your instrument and the rig. If you've ever had the unpleasant experience of touching your guitar and a mic that wasn't connected to a properly grounded circuit, you'll really appreciate the safety factor here.

Cons

→ The signal from your guitar is buffered. Some players just won't accept this, nor will the rig builders who love them.

→ Companding technology in older, analog wireless systems slightly compresses your guitar signal. Metal players won't really notice, and some players will appreciate it, but players with a subtle touch may be bothered by this.

→ Radio interference could impact your tone or cause signal dropouts. Don't worry, though. Your guitar won't suddenly start broadcasting terrestrial radio.

→ Nothing lasts forever. Batteries die. Always use rechargeables.

You may have heard about issues with the 700 MHz frequency spectrum and "White Spaces" impacting wireless users in the US. In 2010 new regulations from the FCC rewrote the rules governing the use of analog broadcasting frequencies, related to the transition to high-definition television broadcasting. For the complete backstory, read the sidebar regarding this topic, but if you're buying a new wireless system, the bottom line is that you don't need to worry about these changes with any of the current wireless products on the market.

700 MHz and White Spaces:
Is Use of Your Wireless Gear Now Illegal?

By Melanie Tolomeo and Scott Kahn
Reprinted courtesy of MusicPlayers.com

The house lights go down and your band takes the stage. It's exciting stuff—you're playing to a capacity crowd, opening up for a touring headliner at the largest concert hall in your home city. The drummer and bassist lay down a wicked groove, and the crowd starts to respond immediately. You flip your amp out of standby and get ready to hit that first power chord. But out of your guitar amp comes a high-pitched voice squealing, "Oh my god, Britney. That singer is so cute!" Meanwhile, you've got no tone whatsoever. "Oh my god. My wireless system has been hijacked by the audience!"

While dramatic, thankfully this isn't what would actually happen. However, interference from new wireless devices may cause wireless signal "dropouts," which are brief (and usually silent) gaps in the signal. You might hear some noise or hiss, but you won't hear what the interfering product is transmitting—which is probably going to be data rather than voice.

Fortunately, recent legislation by the FCC prevents this type of interference-related disaster from happening. However, if you're one of the thousands of gigging musicians in the United States using a wireless system—either for your vocals or your instruments, new changes to the law may have actually made it illegal to use your wireless equipment!

To the astonishment of the entertainment and sports industries, the US government (the FCC in particular) sided with the lobbyists for big businesses, forcing everyone from indie bands to Broadway theaters to houses of worship to pro sports teams to replace much of their existing wireless equipment so that the frequencies this gear used to use could be made available for new services that have nothing to do with the current use of this airspace.

If this was the FCC's attempt at stimulating the economy through forced retail sales, it's a miserable attempt, since for many of us, wireless systems are merely a luxury and not a requirement. Many young bands with limited budgets may have to scrap their existing wireless gear and go back to using cables. The horror!

So just what wireless systems are affected by the new laws? All equipment operating in the 700 MHz frequency space!

The 700 MHz range consists of any frequency between 698 MHz and 806 MHz. Before the US's 2009 switch to digital television (DTV), certain frequencies in this range were used for analog television channels, and others were available for use by wireless systems like your music gear. Prior to January 2010, all wireless systems—including those in the 700 MHz band—required the user to obtain a license. Did you even realize that you were supposed to obtain a license in order to operate your wireless system? Most musicians are blissfully unaware, and the FCC is currently re-evaluating the licensing rules.

Now, with those frequencies no longer in use by television broadcasters, the FCC has allocated that airspace to public safety use, and for companies looking to expand their wireless communication possibilities (that's the corporate greed part). New laws restrict wireless microphones and similar devices from being used in this frequency space so that consumer electronics products not even on the market yet can have free and clear access to this airspace.

All your wireless gear—mics, instrument systems, and in-ear monitors—are essentially tiny radio broadcasting stations. There are government regulations on how strong the radio signal can be; hence most of the wireless products we use only work properly within a range of 100–1,000 feet. Of course every performer in your band or performance group broadcasts on his or her own frequency within the allocated space (unless you're specifically sharing a channel, such as when listening to the same monitor mix).

The Ultra High Frequency (UHF) range was originally 470–806 MHz. Television channels occupied some frequencies in this range, and wireless equipment used the vacant UHF frequencies.

On June 12, 2009, the United States completed its transition to digital television. This switch made channels 2–51 the "core" television channels, and left frequencies 698–806 MHz (or "the 700 MHz range") vacant. The FCC planned that this 108 MHz range would be used for public safety services such as police, ambulance, and fire radio, as well as consumer use.

Why use this frequency space? The 700 MHz range is particularly appealing to developers of mobile devices because it penetrates walls easily—great for rescue personnel. Unfortunately for performers, though, most of the spectrum in the 700 MHz band was auctioned off to private companies such as Google, AT&T, and Verizon (to the tune of billions of dollars) back in March 2008 for their future use. Hoorah! That's government working for the people, right?

The entertainment industry, sadly, can no longer use the 700 MHz band for wireless devices because of the risk of interfering with emergency responders' communications or other new wireless services. In January 2010 the FCC issued a notice that as of June 12, 2010, any wireless microphone equipment that uses frequencies between 698 MHz and 806 MHz is prohibited in the United States.

This gave artists only five months to invest in new equipment. "The short time frame for the 700 MHz transition presents a logistical and financial challenge to musicians who may need to replace equipment to comply with new FCC regulations," says Chris Lyons, manager of Educational and Technical Communications for Shure.

This legislation has the potential to cost the entertainment industry millions of dollars. Any organization that uses wireless microphones, wireless in-ear monitors, wireless audio and video links, and any other similar equipment in the 700 MHz range must purchase new equipment before the deadline, which will have hit by the time you read this.

Groups affected include not only live performers using wireless gear but also broadcasters, sports teams (those familiar Motorola headsets you see on the sidelines at NFL games, for example), and even prayer leaders in places of worship. Some Broadway theaters may not even be able to afford the thousands of dollars' worth of required upgrades. Theater groups aren't very profitable business ventures in the first place.

What Are White Spaces?

The remaining two-thirds of the spectrum, from 470–698 MHz, still contains television channels, but not on every frequency. Between the stations are "white spaces," where wireless microphones and similar equipment can lawfully operate, with a priority secondary only to television itself. Plenty of gear, such as the very popular Shure SLX and ULX series, use this white space.

But lobbyists are threatening the entertainment business's ownership of this space too. The FCC made the decision (under the major lobbying influence of companies such as Verizon) to allow unlicensed devices to use the white spaces in this range for a new generation of mobile devices (possibly laptops, PDAs, portable game devices, cell phones, etc.). This has huge potential to interfere with wireless music systems.

If hundreds or thousands of fans at a concert or theater performance are carrying new wireless electronic devices—what Google executive Richard Whitt called "Wi-Fi on steroids" (http://googlepublicpolicy.blogspot.com/2009/02/introducing-white-spaces-database-group.html)—operating on the same frequency as your wireless guitar system, good luck finding a free frequency space for your wireless systems.

Is My Gear Even Usable Anymore? What Should I Buy?

Unfortunately, despite efforts from an industry coalition led by Shure and other companies lobbying against the 700 MHz Order, the legislation has been passed.

Find out if your wireless microphone system operates within the restricted bands here: http://www.fcc.gov/cgb/wirelessmicrophones/manufacturers.html.

If your wireless microphone/instrument/monitoring system operates in the 698–806 MHz range, you are now prohibited by law from using this equipment in the United States. Your only option is to invest in new equipment that operates in a different frequency space.

Digital wireless products such as the Line 6 Relay systems operate in the 2.4 GHz band and are unaffected by the new legislation, and new in-ear monitoring systems like the Shure PSM 900 (and many of their other systems) use frequencies below the 700 MHz space.

If you're purchasing new wireless gear, be sure to thoroughly research what frequency space the equipment operates in. If it works in the white space area—470–698 MHz—you're in the clear for now. But be aware that in the future, you might need to upgrade to products using a different range, as more consumer products compete for those frequencies.

To help defray the cost of new wireless gear, many manufacturers of wireless systems for musicians are offering trade-in rebates toward the purchase of new, compliant wireless systems, but those deals won't exist forever. At least now when you're justifying your gear purchase to a significant other you can say, "I have no choice. The government is forcing me to do this." *Hmmm*, that certainly sounds like a tax-deductible expense to us!

If you're new to wireless technology, I caution you against purchasing a used system unless it's a current-generation product. Many older systems are now illegal to operate in the United States, not to mention that they don't sound as good as the current products.

Signal dropouts are extremely rare with pro systems, as their multiple antennas and supporting technology do a great job of making sure that a strong signal is always being received.

For all the debate about audio quality with wired vs. wireless, consider that many pros are still touring with wireless systems that aren't even taking advantage of the latest advancements in analog or digital wireless technology. In real world use, you will not hear any difference between a wired and wireless signal. You can still roll off your volume knob and hear the character of your tube amp change. It's only in a studio-quiet A/B test that you might notice a difference.

Placement of Wireless Systems in Your Rack

There is one very important concern with wireless units: their placement in your rig. If you have a rackmounted preamp or power amp, placing your wireless receiver in close proximity to your amp can result in noticeable noise or other electrical interference, and you could spend hours trying to isolate the noise problem before realizing it can easily be fixed.

In many of my rigs, I routinely installed wireless receivers just above my preamps without any issues, but in my most recent rig, the placement of the wireless unit caused a horrible amount of interference. By simply reversing the mounting of the half-rack-size receiver so it was above the opposite side of my preamp (farther away from its power transformer), the noise problem went away.

Many pro rigs keep their multiple wireless systems in separate racks from their amps and effects, but until you have a team of guys moving your gear around, you'll probably be keeping everything in a single rack.

Additionally, if your wireless unit did not include a set of front-mounting antennas, you'll want to purchase that before installing the wireless system in your rack. If your antenna is buried deep inside a big shock rack, expect its range to be significantly reduced.

Products of Interest: Wireless Instrument Systems

Line 6 Relay G90, G55, G30

Fig. 10.21: Line6 G90

Thc Line 6 Relay G90 makes a great digital wireless choice for use in building your professional guitar rig without breaking the bank. You get 10 Hz–20 kHz frequency response, 120 dB of dynamic range, 24-bit A/D converters, up to a 300-foot range, and great sound. It installs into a single rack space, and it operates in the 2.4 GHz ISM frequency space (a good place to be).

The TBP12 transmitter runs on AA batteries (invest in rechargeable batteries since they only last eight to ten hours) and uses an industry standard TA4F-style locking connector where the cable meets the transmitter. You can purchase premium cables with a choice of straight- or right-angle jacks and Mogami wire from the Line 6 website, which I suggest doing. Keep a spare in your gig bag or rack drawer.

Fig. 10.22: Line 6 G55

The newest Relay product, the G55, is a half-rack unit that delivers the G90's performance while barely sacrificing some high-end openness, as dynamic range here is only 117 dB. Rackmount hardware has been announced, and a pair of these could prove useful in a variety of situations (for example, electric guitars with piezo acoustic outputs).

The G50 is a rugged stomp box–sized wireless system that you can install on your pedalboard. It delivers the same audio specs as the G90 but with a shorter maximum distance of 200 feet. It also has an interesting cable tone feature, which lets you simulate the effect of longer instrument cable runs by rolling off some of the high frequencies. Why would you choose to do this? If you gig sometimes wired and sometimes wirelessly, you can dial in a wireless tone that better matches your wired tone, so you never have to mess with your amp's EQ.

Shure ULXD14 and GLXD6

The Shure ULXD14 system is what you'll want for the headlining world tour. It integrates with network-managed Shure wireless systems for large-scale touring productions, and I love that it uses rechargeable lithium-ion batteries. Just drop the transmitter into a charging cradle—no need to pull batteries out or plug cables!

Fig. 10.23: Line 6 G50

Fig. 10.24: Shure ULXD

The system features 20 Hz–20 kHz frequency range, 120 dB dynamic range, and encrypted transmission of the audio transmission, and it includes a rackmount kit that will let you install a pair of these side by side in 1U of rack space with the antennas moved to the front. A/D conversion is 24-bit/48 kHz. ULX-series equipment is on the pricier side by musician standards, and I'm hoping that Shure introduces an SLX-series digital instrument system, as that product line hit the sweet spot for price/performance in "typical" pro guitar rigs with analog wireless systems.

Fig. 10.25: Shure GLXD6

The Shure GLXD6 is going to end up on a ton of pedalboards by the time this book hits the street. Sure (ahem), it looks an awful lot like the Line 6 Relay G50 sans the antennas (they're built in, and the range is 200 feet). And specs-wise, it's in the same ballpark as the Relay. But the GLXD6 changes the game by including an on-board tuner! That alone sets the wireless system apart because now we get a rugged, pro-quality wireless system for our pedalboards that includes a tuner (with a Carling-style footswitch that mutes the output for silent tuning). One fewer pedal on the board can make all the difference when space is at a premium. And the tuner works great, at least in my limited use with six-string guitars tuned close to pitch (i.e., I can't vouch for you metal guys tuning down to dropped A).

The GLXD6 system has a 20 Hz–20 kHz frequency range and 24-bit/44.1 kHz A/D, and it also operates in the 2.4 GHz range. The specs keep getting better, though, because this is the first reasonably priced, pro-spec'd wireless system that includes a lithium-ion rechargeable battery! And like Line 6, Shure uses industry standard TA4F-style locking connectors for their instrument cables, so it's easy to upgrade with premium cables (though the Shure cables are particularly nice in the first place).

Also Consider

There are numerous wireless systems on the market today. You might want to check out the Sony DWZB30GB DWZ Series or Audio-Technica's System 10. The System 10 wireless system sounds great and is dirt cheap, but it's not rackmountable, so it's not the best solution for a professional guitar rig at this time. Sony's system can fit on your pedalboard.

There are numerous analog systems available, but at this time, I am no longer going to recommend any of them (as I did in the first edition of this book). The digital systems sound better, and by the time you get your hands on this book, we may have new professional digital wireless solutions to consider from companies including Sennheiser and Lectrasonics, too.

Cabling

A book like this would be incomplete without a discussion of cabling. You weren't seriously going to wire up your racks with off-the-shelf cables, were you? You certainly can do this, and the advantage is you'll have high-quality, reliable, soldered cables in your rig.

However, I want your rig to be nice and tidy like the pro rigs we're talking about. This requires custom cabling solutions, and many of you have already explored some of these solutions when wiring up pedalboards.

Fig. 10.26: If only we could wire our own rigs as neatly as Mark Snyder does for John Petrucci!

The most widely used custom cabling kits are manufactured by George L's, Planet Waves, and Lava Cable. The kits include a length of premium quality, uncut cable and straight or right-angle connectors that are typically connected in a solderless manner either by tightening by hand or using tiny screws.

Be warned: making custom cables can easily lead to hours of frustration and troubleshooting if you don't have a decent cable tester handy during assembly (that's a device, not your buddy). Ron Menelli of RJM Music

Technology gets right to the point on this topic: "Testing is critical and practice is essential to make solderless cables correctly. Test every cable. Don't assume that any cable you make will work the first time. It gets easier with practice. If the cable is going to get moved at all, I wouldn't use anything other than soldered connectors, but on a pedalboard or in a rack where the wiring is somewhat protected, solderless can be okay."

I had a 50 percent success rate the first time I began assembling some George L's custom cables. Test your custom cables!

The other thing to consider when wiring up your rack: minimizing electrical crosstalk that might yield noise in your audio signal from the electrical power cords. Whenever possible, run power cables down one side of your rack and audio cables down the other. Where power and audio cables must interact, it's always best for your cables to cross each other at right angles.

Custom Rack Interfaces

Fig. 10.27: Many rig builders put custom patchbays into pro rigs to simplify hook-up and teardown.

You may have noticed various cable patchbays installed in pro rigs and wondered how they fit into the rig architecture. In many of the pro touring rigs, these interfaces are custom designed specifically for each rig. They serve two principal purposes:

→ To make it fast and brain-dead simple to connect the various components in a guitar rig to each other. Commonly, the jacks are color coded and/or numbered, as are all connecting cables. Your tech doesn't have time to worry about connection accidents when you're playing a festival show and he's got ten minutes to move your rig to the stage and get it up and running.

Also, the last thing anyone needs is to have to dig into the back of a rack to find the right place to connect a cable when the stage is dark. These panels commonly provide a simple way of moving the jacks buried inside the rig to an easy access location on the front or back of the rack.

→ Protecting your gear. Constantly plugging/unplugging the components in your rig leads to real wear and tear on the jacks and connection points. Instead, have your crew plug and unplug your rack cables on a patchbay, whose jacks can be easily serviced if something breaks. Having to remove your rack gear and open it up just to change out a faulty input/ouput jack is far too time-consuming and risky before show time.

All of the custom rig builders rely on parts from companies including Neutrik, Amphenol, Switchcraft, and Belden. All you need is a blank rack panel, a couple of jacks, a soldering iron, and a custom cable kit or two, and you can create an interface that suits your own rig. In Fig. 10.27 above, a custom interface was even built into a small electrical box attached to the edge of a pedalboard.

An Internet search will yield a wide range of industrial manufacturers that can easily build custom rack panels and breakout boxes for the connectors of your choice. Or you can have custom rig-building companies build interfaces that meet your specific design criteria.

If your needs are simple—you just need to move some jacks from your gear to the front or back of your rack, custom rack panels are a nice do-it-yourself type of project to undertake. If your entire rig exists in a single rack, a custom interface may be unnecessary.

Products of Interest

Rackman makes a variety of rack panels with Neutrik "D" style cutouts already in them, and Whirlwind sells a variety of rack panels with your choice of XLR or ¼-inch punch-outs, some with optional enclosure boxes.

You can also buy blank rack panels and drill your own holes if you're motivated enough to build your own custom interfaces. Just create the panel you need, purchase some connectors, solder some wire, and you're all set! The aforementioned Neutrik D family of connectors is widely used by rig builders.

Raxxess Metalsmiths can custom drill the panel of your dreams. Design your panel in Adobe Illustrator or Photoshop and send it to them for a custom quote.

Dutch company DAP Audio (a division of Highlite International BV) manufactures a wide variety of blank panels, ventilated panels, and punched panels.

Rack Cases

Now that you're ready to build a rack for your rig, it's time to find the *right* rack. They come in a wide range of sizes and materials, and offer different features that matter more or less to different players.

Most racks are built from plywood of differing thickness (anywhere from 3/8 inch to ½ inch to ¾ inch), which directly influences how heavy the rack is and how much protection it offers. Larger, heavier racks typically have casters, making it easy to roll them around, and handles on the sides for lifting.

Fig. 10.28: Steve Stevens's rig includes shock racks for his tube amp heads, a standard rack for effects, and a lightweight SKB case for his wireless units.

Companies like SKB Case and Gator build rack cases out of polymer (plastic) materials that weigh a fraction as much as wooden cases, yet offer similar protection. Although these are great for local gigs, most touring rigs use wooden cases (covered in laminate or carpet), though we have seen many of SKB's shock-mounted cases in touring rigs. These shock racks are constructed from significantly heavier-duty materials than the lightweight plastic cases you are most likely familiar with (and consequently they aren't that much lighter than some wooden rack cases). *Note: I'm not talking about specialty cases for mixers or instrument cases; only rack cases for holding your rackmounted guitar gear.*

Shock racks offer the best protection for sensitive equipment like tube amps. These oversized racks are essentially racks inside of racks. Your equipment screws into the interior rack, and that rack is suspended either inside a layer of high-density foam or on a spring/coil suspension inside an exterior case shell. Both shock-mount solutions work well, providing fantastic isolation from bumps and drops, but shock racks are larger, heavier, and far more expensive than non-shock racks. However, if you're doing any touring, and especially if other people will be carting your gear around, I must stress the importance of using a shock rack to hold your delicate tube-based gear or other sensitive equipment.

Fig. 10.29: This SKB shock case weighs almost as much as a non-shock wooden case, and it protects your guitar rig by suspending the 19-inch equipment rack inside the outer case.

Rack sizes are measured in space *units* (U)—each unit is 1.75 inches tall. A 4U rack is one that has four rack spaces for gear. A typical multi-effects processor is 1U or 2U tall, which designates how much space it will take up in a rack.

You can assemble a small rack with a power conditioner, multi-effects processor, and wireless receiver quite easily. A small 3U or 4U rack doesn't weigh much and is very portable. In fact, you can buy some small racks built right into nylon-covered gig bags—check out the Gator GRB Rack Bag if you need one of these.

If you're building a large rig—ten spaces or more—numerous custom case builders can build cases to your precise specs and colors. An Internet search will reveal builders including Calzone Case, Rock Hard, Maxline, Middle Atlantic, New York Case Company, Road Runner, and more. But there are also plenty of large racks available from big companies like Calzone and SKB that don't require custom orders. You'll save some money if one of these builders has a large case that fits your needs sitting in its inventory.

When you're ready to rack your head, or even your speaker cabinets and combos, you'll definitely want to talk with the custom case builders. It's common for pros to tour with cases that hold multiple amp heads and rack gear together. Just pop the doors off, run a few cables, and you're ready to rock.

Fig. 10.30: This Calzone case has a shock-protected compartment for a guitar amplifier, and space for rack gear and storage above. Note that heads are typically mounted in the bottom of custom cases for weight distribution purposes.

Custom rack cases also make it easy to add custom features, whether it's a drawer in the bottom of the case to hold your spare tubes and cables or a custom light show that makes your rig look like something from the bridge of the Death Star. You would be surprised at how many cases are ordered with bottle openers attached! Regrettably, though, I haven't found any good custom shock rack cases that include free roadie support.

Drawers and Shelves

One of the coolest things about having a drawer in your rig is that it gives you a convenient place to stash all your rock 'n' roll essentials: spare guitar strings, tools, spare cables, spare tubes, batteries, your wireless transmitter, your in-ear monitors, cleaning rag, and more.

When you custom order a case, it's easy to get drawers built right into the rig. A large drawer that runs the entire dimensions of your rack case can easily hold your MIDI foot controller or other pedalboard, making it easy to keep your entire rig together in one place.

Rack shelves are a good place to stash your pedals, but you'll typically lose an extra 2U–3U of space in your rack to accommodate the shelf with pedals on top, so factor that in when planning your rack.

Fig. 10.31: Custom cases from Calzone, Maxline, and Rock Hard. Maxline's drawer, which spans the entire bottom of the rig, can accommodate large MIDI foot controllers or pedalboards.

Products of Interest

There are numerous suppliers of rack accessories, but the most widely available drawers and shelves, and blank rack panels to fill in the gaps, come from Raxxess Metalsmiths, Middle Atlantic Products, Gator, and SKB.

Random Goodies: Things You Didn't Know You Could Get for Your Rig

In this section, I've collected a few items that didn't fall neatly into the other chapters in this book. As you'll discover, if you can dream something up for your rig, there's a good chance that someone has already built the product for you. Listing the full range of specialized pedals and accessories would warrant another book or two, so consider this just the tiniest sampling of what's available. Be sure to visit the websites of the companies mentioned in this book to discover many solutions for building custom rigs.

Products of Interest

Musicom Lab MVC MIDI Volume Controller

Fig. 10.32: Musicom
Lab MVC

I hate long cable runs on the floor that add limited value, so this gadget from
Musicom Lab is a real blessing for players who like volume pedals. Stick it in
your rack and run your guitar instrument cable into it rather than into your
amp. Then connect a short cable from the MVC to your input jack. Hook up
a MIDI cable, and your foot controller's continuous controller pedal can
be used as a volume pedal, digitally controlling the all-analog VCA circuit
and eliminating the need to run an additional long cable from your setup.
Alternatively, you could place it in your effects loop, depending on your
preference for placement of a volume control.

Sound Sculpture Volcano MIDI and Expression
Pedal Controlled Volume

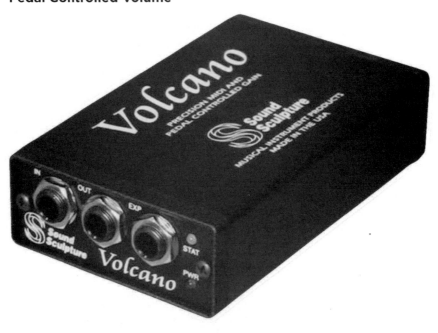

Fig. 10.33: Sound
Sculpture Volcano

Volcano takes a different approach to volume control. Unlike the Musicom Lab MVC, which is meant to work exclusively with MIDI-controlled continuous controllers, you connect a volume or expression pedal directly to the Volcano, along with the input and output from your guitar and your amp. Without connecting any MIDI cables, the Volcano can function as an analog volume solution, keeping the audio path inside the box and not running down the cable to your physical volume pedal.

Rather than using a VCA circuit, the Volcano uses resistors for level control, and you can flip some switches inside the Volcano to custom tweak the volume range to 0 dB, boost, or cut. It accepts both instrument- and line-level signals, so feel free to stick it in your effects loop if that's more useful to you.

When connected to your MIDI rig, it gives you the ability to save specific volume levels to individual presets, as well as to control volume from a continuous controller over MIDI.

Axess Electronics BS2 Guitar Audio Buffer/Splitter

This simple box has one guitar input, a buffered circuit, and three outputs, allowing you to split your signal between a tuner and up to two amps. There is an isolated transformer and phase-reverse switch for the second amp.

Fig. 10.34: Axess Electronics BS2

Radial Engineering BigShot EFX True Bypass Effects Switcher

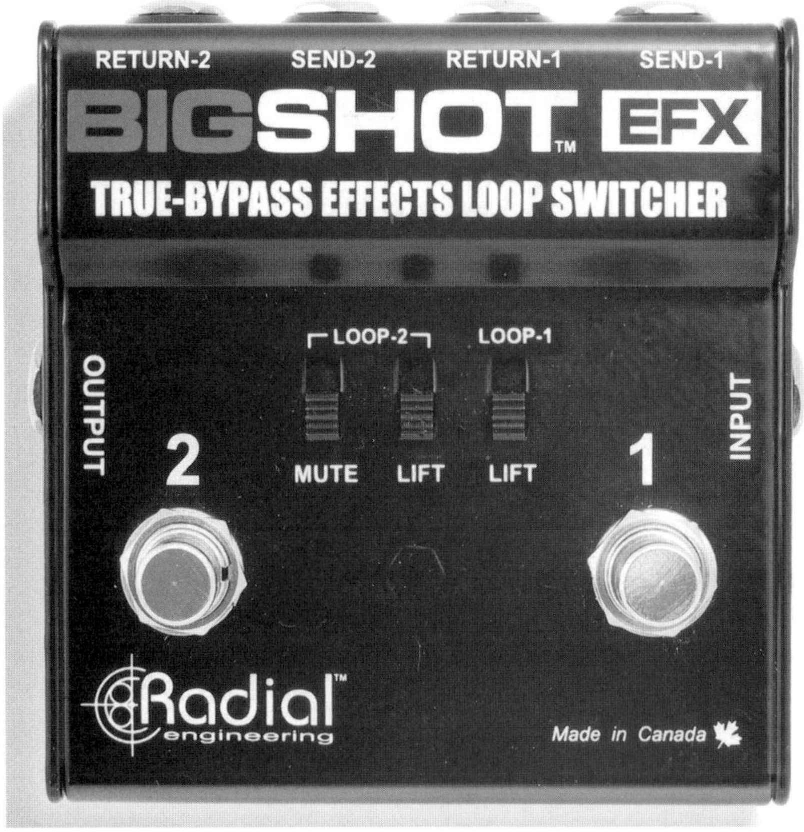

Fig. 10.35: Radial
Engineering
BigShot EFX

This true-bypass pedal lets you add two series loops to your rig wherever you'd like them to go, either in front of your amp or in the effects loop. It has an optional buffer, and placing a few pedals in each loop gives you single-button on/bypass control. Or place a tuner in the second loop if you lack a dedicated tuner output elsewhere in your rig.

RJM Music Tone Saver

Fig. 10.36: RJM
ToneSaver

The Tone Saver is a very simple, pedal-sized buffer that utilizes the same circuitry found in other RJM Music Technology products. It has a second isolated output, so you can split your signal to two amps or to a tuner.

Robert Keeley Electronics Looper

The super-compact Looper pedal turns any of your pedals into a true-bypass pedal! If you want to take your buffered BOSS pedal, for example, and completely remove it from your signal path, just hook it up to the Looper, which becomes your new on/bypass switch for the pedal.

Fig. 10.37: Robert Keeley Looper

Visual Sound Time Bandit

This is a fantastic utility device that will find a home in many professional guitar rigs (not to mention studios). If you love to use time-based effects, this $120 accessory is a no-brainer. It functions in two different ways: In BPM mode, you simply connect it to the tap tempo pedal input on your delay or other time-based effect and dial in the BPM you need on the dial, and it outputs tap tempo to your effect. In Click Track mode, you connect the output from your mixing board or laptop DAW's click track and connect that to the pedal's input jack, and then the Time Bandit converts the click track to tap temp and outputs the tempo to your effect's tap tempo input jack. Sweet!

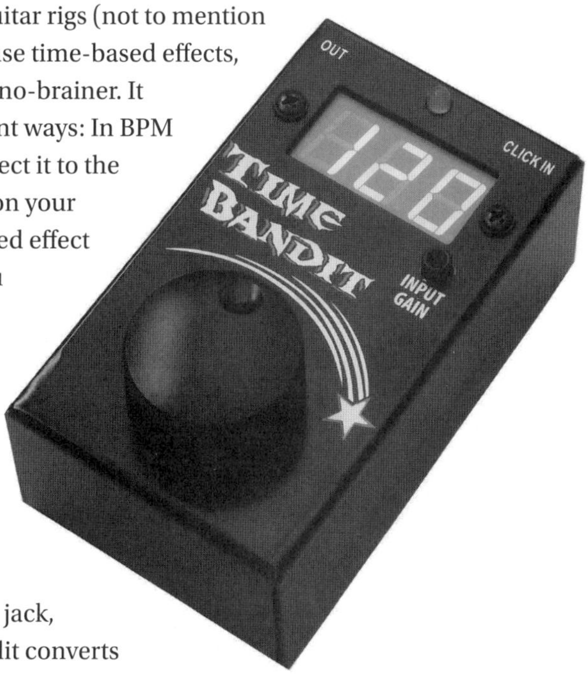

Fig. 10.38: Visual Sound Time Bandit.

CHAPTER 11

Suggested Uses and Rig Examples

Rather than create my own illustrations showing how various components in a pro rig work together, this chapter begins with diagrams supplied by the manufacturers of rig-building products and ends with an in-depth look at the guitar rigs of some pretty well-known players. If you're still with me this far into the book, you'll find that these illustrations and their accompanying notes should paint a great picture of how you can begin using these items in your rig.

As you will discover, rack gear isn't used by every pro with a big guitar sound. You'll see some great rig designs built around a large pedalboard or two. In fact, the various pros whose rigs are explored in this chapter each have very different methods of using their gear. Some guys like to step on lots of pedals, while others like to automate everything down to a single button stomp. But what all of their rigs have in common is a desire to keep the signal path as clean and quiet as possible, using loopers and mixers wherever possible so that when a piece of equipment isn't in use, the guitar signal isn't passing through it.

Suggested Uses of Popular Products

These examples show only a particular application of certain products that were discussed in greater detail earlier in the book, but each product can be used in numerous additional ways. Be sure to visit www.musicplayers.com/mgr and the manufacturers' websites to learn other ways to implement these products.

Radial Engineering JX-44: Many Guitars, Many Amps

In this example, four wireless systems connect to the JX-44, and four guitar amps connect to the outputs. A tuner is connected, multiple effects are shared via the JX-44's effects loop, and the DI runs to a mixing board. Two foot controllers are used with the JX-44: one for selecting guitars and one for selecting amps.

The nice thing about the JX-44's dual pedal inputs is that your guitar tech can select the operational guitar after s/he hands you an instrument for your next song, but onstage, you just select which amp you're playing through.

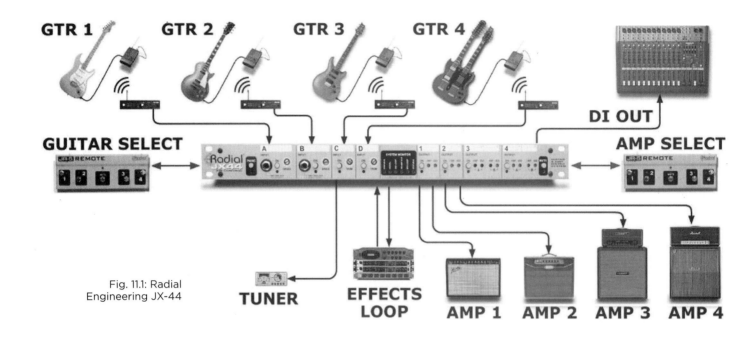

Fig. 11.1: Radial Engineering JX-44

Guitar Laboratory GSC-3: Pedalboard Looper and MIDI Control

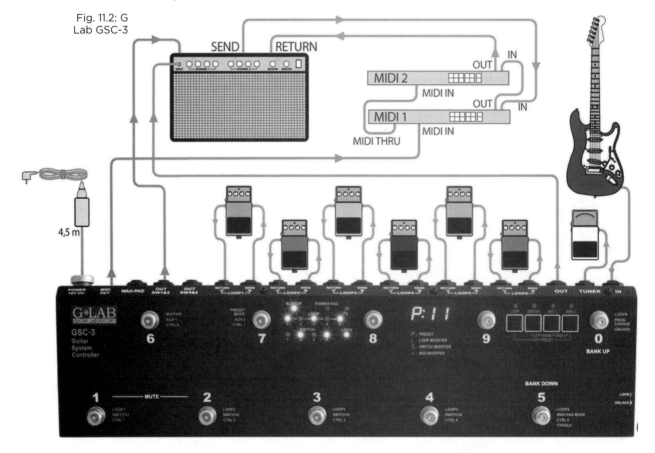

Fig. 11.2: G Lab GSC-3

The GSC-3 simplifies cleaning up your signal chain on the floor. In this example, six effects pedals are placed in their own audio loops, and a tuner is connected to a dedicated output. A pair of rackmounted signal processors—perhaps a delay and reverb unit—run in the amp's effects loop, and MIDI control from the GSC-3 enables selection of effects presets. Additionally, the first switch output on the GSC-3 is used to control channel selection on the amp.

With this elegant and compact solution, a single button press can enable multiple individual pedals, set the rack gear to specific presets (or bypass that gear if it supports a bypass function controlled via MIDI CC messages), and set your amp to its clean or heavy channel.

Voodoo Lab GCX: Pedals, Multiple Switches, and Creative Effects Loop Control

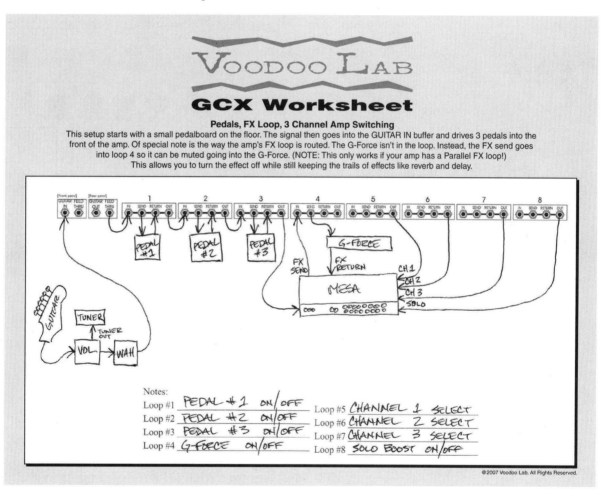

Fig. 11.3: Voodoo Lab GCX

This example features a three-channel Mesa/Boogie Rectifier series amp and the Voodoo Lab GCX. The signal flows from a guitar to floor pedals—volume and wah (with a tuner in the sidechain output from the volume pedal). These pedals run into the buffered input circuit and are followed by a few more pedals connected to individual audio loops, after which the signal goes into the amp's instrument input jack.

Rather than running the TC Electronic G-Force multi-effects processor directly in the amp's effect loop, the G-Force is connected to an audio loop—but only the signal input. In this way, you can play a sound with long delay repeats or reverb tails, and after you bypass the loop, you can keep on playing a tight sound without the G-Force, but the repeats and reverberation continue until they decay naturally.

Four switches are connected to the GCX from the amp, allowing you to select the three different amp channels and also control the amp's Solo/Boost feature.

RJM Music Technology Rack Gizmo and Mini Line Mixer: Big Rig Made Easy

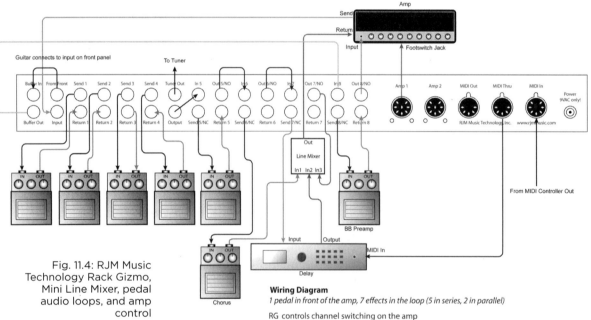

Fig. 11.4: RJM Music Technology Rack Gizmo, Mini Line Mixer, pedal audio loops, and amp control

In this example, there is only one pedal in front of the amp—an Xotic Guitars BB preamp—but there are multiple pedals and rack effects in the effects loop. Complete control of the amp and its various function switches is also provided.

After the amp's Effects Send enters the RAck Gizmo, the first five effects connected to the Rack Gizmo run in series, but the chorus and rackmounted delay unit run in parallel loops. The output of the five-pedal series, chorus, and delay go into the Mini Line Mixer, and its output goes to the Effects Return on the amp. Because only the input to the delay unit comes from the Rack Gizmo (not the output), bypassing the loop doesn't cut off delay repeats.

Custom Audio Electronics Dual/Stereo Mini Mixer

One look at the Dual/Stereo Mini Mixer example from CAE and a few of you may scratch your heads at this suggested setup. It had me running back to my rig to experiment with effect placement after talking about it with Bob Bradshaw.

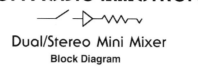

CUSTOM AUDIO ELECTRONICS

Dual/Stereo Mini Mixer
Block Diagram

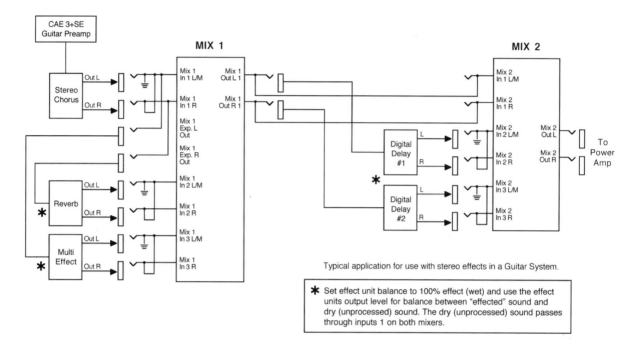

Typical application for use with stereo effects in a Guitar System.

✱ Set effect unit balance to 100% effect (wet) and use the effect units output level for balance between "effected" sound and dry (unprocessed) sound. The dry (unprocessed) sound passes through inputs 1 on both mixers.

The example starts with the output from a CAE 3+SE rackmounted guitar preamp, but you can substitute your own preamp or the effects send from any amp. The output runs into a stereo chorus effect (rack or pedal, but hopefully one with some great audio specs), and from there the stereo outputs run into Mix 1 in the DSMM.

A reverb unit and multi-effects processor run in parallel to each other, with a mono signal feeding each unit (the left or right side of the stereo output from the chorus effect).

The stereo output of the reverb and multi-effects processor feed Mix 2 in the DSMM, and there are two stereo digital delay units running in parallel within Mix 2. At first, this arrangement threw me for a loop as I have always preached placing delay in front of reverb, but in a parallel system like this, I understand Bob Bradshaw's design philosophy: "If the delays are before reverb, or in parallel, the repeats decay with whatever comes before them, that is, dry sound. If the reverb decay is longer than the delay repeats (and typically is), I suppose reverb at the end of the chain works to a certain extent. But if the reverb decay is relatively short, it sounds more natural to me for the delay to be *after*."

Output from Mix 2 runs to a power amp, or could run into your amp's stereo effects return. The entire setup could easily be run in mono if using the mono loop on a typical amp.

Fig. 11.5: Custom Audio Electronics Dual/Stereo Line Mixer and multiple effects

Rig Examples

Following is an in-depth look at some great guitar rigs. Whether these belong to your favorite guitar hero or a player you're not really familiar with, one thing becomes quite clear: there is no single "right" way to build a pro rig. You will find players debating rig design methods to death in online forums, but as you'll see from this assortment of outstanding players, the right pro rig is the one that works intuitively the way *you* think about your rig.

To see the fine details, high-resolution color photos are available at http://musicplayers.com/mgr.

Alex Lifeson

Builders: Scott Appleton (amp rack and wireless rack) and Mark Snyder (effects rack)

Fig. 11.6: Alex Lifeson's rig

As the legendary guitar player for the band Rush, Alex Lifeson has a huge guitar sound that sometimes makes it seem as if there is more than one of him onstage playing. Rest assured it's all live Alex, just helped here and there by some cool technology.

Alex's guitar rig is an interesting one in that it features many of the typical capabilities of a modern rig, but he chooses to operate most of it in an old-school, stomp box style.

Holy wireless! Alex's rig has one entire rack filled with wireless receivers, the majority from Audio-Technica and a pair from Lectrosonics. Two of Alex's Gibson Les Paul guitars are equipped with TonePros bridges loaded with piezo acoustic elements. Since the magnetic pickups output their signal to the guitar rig and the piezo output goes to the PA system, each of those guitars requires two wireless transmitters/receivers.

A second pair of wireless units is always standing by, connected to the next guitar Alex will switch to during a set, while another pair remains as a backup in case of problems with the other units. Then below the Audio-Technica receivers sit a pair of Lectrasonics wireless units for Alex's acoustic guitars.

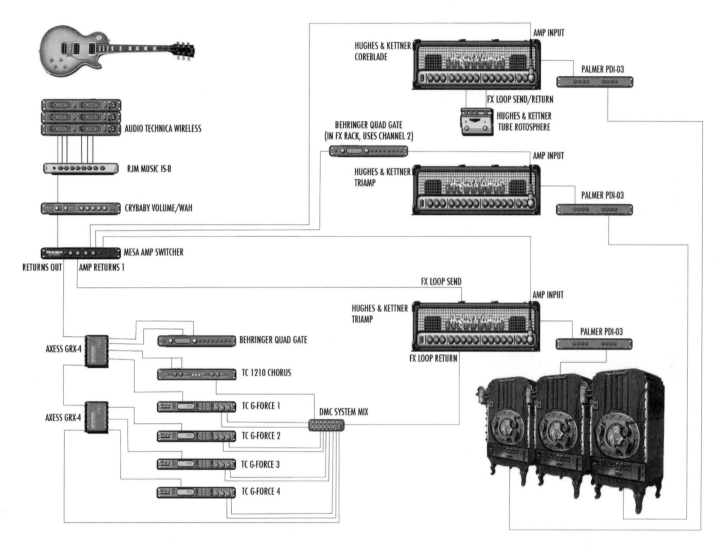

Fig. 11.7: Alex Lifeson's electric guitar rig

Reviewing Alex's rig diagrams, you can see that the guitar signals from the six Audio-Technica wireless receivers feed an RJM Music Technology IS-8. This custom-order product (RJM built these for Green Day and Rascal Flatts, too) looks similar to an Amp Gizmo and features eight inputs and four outputs, where all of the inputs send identical signals to each of the outputs.

One output goes to a rackmounted Dunlop Cry Baby wah pedal. Alex's pedalboard features two continuous controller pedals next to his MIDI foot controller. One of these controls the familiar Cry Baby wah sounds, and the other one controls a VCA circuit in the Cry Baby unit that is used for volume control over the entire rig. The output from the Cry Baby goes into a Mesa/Boogie High Gain Amp Switch, which not only lets you route signals to four different amps, but also has a dedicated effects loop.

From the Mesa/Boogie Amp Switch, the signal is routed to three guitar amps: two Hughes & Kettner Triamp Mk II Alex Lifeson signature heads, and one Hughes & Kettner Coreblade.

→ The first Triamp is run totally dry, and the incoming signal first passes through one channel of a Behringer XR4400 Multigate Pro noise gate. The amp's output goes into a Palmer PDI-03 speaker simulator and then into a Hughes & Kettner Statesman STM 212 2x12 speaker cabinet hidden inside one of the retro sci-fi cabinets on stage (all three of those creations contain 212 cabinets; one for each of the amps in the rig).

→ The second Triamp also outputs to a Palmer PDI-03 and STM212 cabinet, but this "wet" head runs all of Alex's effects through its effects loop. The loop in this amp can be run in series or parallel, but it's 100 percent wet (series) for this rig since parallel mixing of effects happens elsewhere in the signal chain.

→ The FX Loop Send goes back to the Mesa/Boogie HGAS, and from there to the amp switcher's effects loop. The HGAS Returns Output sends a signal to the first (of two) Axess Electronics GRX-4 audio looper.

→ All signals pass through a Behringer XR4400 Multigate Pro noise gate.

→ The remaining loops in the two GRX-4 loopers contain a TC Electronic 1210 chorus and four TC Electronic G-Force multi-effects processors. Alex typically runs two delays in the majority of his playing, and the first two G-Force units are dedicated to running individual delays. The third G-Force is used for reverbs and occasional pitch-shifting effects, and the fourth G-Force is dedicated to a specific flanger effect. Putting each of these effects processors in loops in the GRX-4 ensures that when an effect isn't in use, it's completely out of the signal chain.

→ The output from all of the effects devices goes into a Digital Music Corp System Mix, a stereo line mixer no longer in production but still widely used. The output of the mixer goes into the FX Loop Return on the wet Triamp head. One significant change to Alex's rig on the 2010–2011 Time Machine tour is that his entire rig is being run in mono. But if Alex wanted to run it in stereo, it would be virtually as simple as connecting a second output from the System Mix and running that to the Return on a second wet Triamp head and into another speaker cabinet.

So what about that Hughes & Kettner Coreblade with the Rotosphere effect in its dedicated effects loop? This amp is the "secret sauce" in the rig. Alex can add this amp as an additional layer when needed, and many listeners have been fooled by its presence in the mix, thinking there must be someone else playing another guitar part. The Coreblade has onboard effects, and Alex makes use of them when adding additional textures. For the die-hard fan, the most obvious use of this amp is during the end of the guitar solo in the song "Limelight," where Alex has a delay trail that seems to go on and on after he's moved on to play the next section of the song. Kick in the Coreblade, play the ending note of the solo with a huge delay from the internal effects, and then kick that amp out of the loop. The sound repeats, but Alex is already playing the final chorus. Cool! Other times he'll kick this amp in for an additional heavy layer to thicken up part of a song. Listen for it the next time you're watching the band in concert.

Alex's acoustic guitar rig is simpler than the electric side of things. The

ALEX' PIEZO RIG

GIBSON LES PAUL EQUIPPED WITH
A FISHMAN POWERBIRDGE

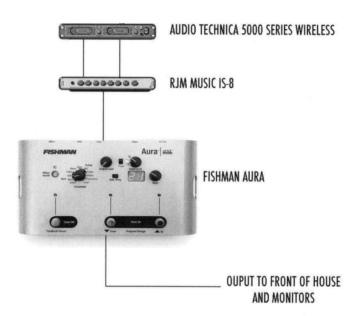

AUDIO TECHNICA 5000 SERIES WIRELESS

RJM MUSIC IS-8

FISHMAN AURA

OUPUT TO FRONT OF HOUSE
AND MONITORS

Fig. 11.8: Alex Lifeson's
piezo guitar rig

piezo acoustic output from his Les Paul guitars runs into a pair of Audio-
Technica wireless units, into a second RJM IS-8, and then into a Fishman
Aura signal processor, which lets Alex apply modeled acoustic tones to the
acoustic instrument source.

On songs where Alex plays an actual acoustic guitar or mandolin, those
wireless units run straight into the PA system.

Controlling this guitar rig is where Alex's "old school" approach comes
into play. The custom foot controller in front of the Axess Electronics FX1
MIDI controller selects channels on the Triamp guitar amplifiers, and there
are two variants on the tone for each channel (A and B), while the last button
enables or disables the effects loop for silent tuning with the BOSS tuner on
the floor.

On each side of the pedalboard is a footswitch with a red status diode.
This switch enables the piezo output from Alex's guitars, and the two are
clones of each other so that Alex can get immediate access to his acoustic
tone no matter where he's standing in relation to the pedalboard.

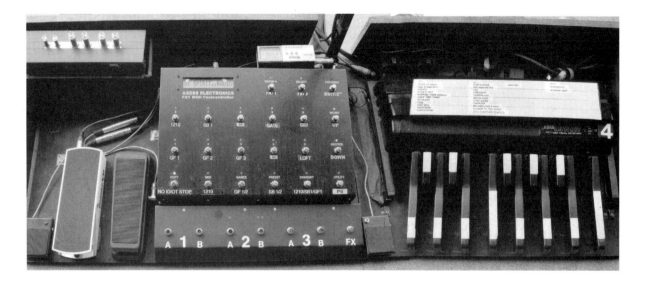

Fig. 11.9: Alex Lifeson's pedalboard

The FX1 changes Alex's effects settings, and all of the buttons are assigned to a single song, or scene, at a time. Using the Up/Down buttons on the right side of the controller, Alex scrolls from song to song and then steps on the "No Idiot Stop" button, which sends all of the necessary MIDI Program Change (PC) and Continuous Controller (CC) messages to set all desired effects properly for the current song.

Buttons labeled GF1, GF2, and GF3 let Alex enable or bypass his individual G-Force multi-effects processors, which are each dedicated to a single task in most songs. The 1210 button enables or bypasses the TC Electronic chorus unit, and the SB1/2 button lets Alex kick in the Coreblade amplifier when he needs it. Other buttons enable him to instantly bypass all of his effects, while some of the first-row buttons duplicate individual features from above so that Alex doesn't have to perform a delicate balancing act, stepping on second- or third-row buttons, which are actually quite a long way away from his feet, since the FX1 is situated above his amp's channel selector.

Sure, the rig could be more easily automated and the custom footswitch in front removed, but Alex prefers this "real amp" approach (dare we call it the "free will" approach?). After the FX1 has dialed up all of his effects for a song, he can freely step on clean channels or dirty channels without ever risking any of the latency or delays introduced by a complex switching system.

The classic Korg MIDI pedals are used for playing or triggering keyboard parts, while the strange box in the top left corner of the pedalboard is a super-secret, holy grail, sound-shaping preamp that takes the entire rig and makes it sound like a transistor radio. Just kidding—it's actually a tube clock and is just for show . . . and for knowing what time it is, of course!

John Petrucci

Builders: Mark Snyder and Matthew "Maddi" Schieferstein

If you're a big fan of Dream Theater's John Petrucci, you know that he typically has a pretty big Mesa/Boogie guitar rig or two behind him, loaded up with classic effects like the TC Electronic 2290 delay and modern switching systems from companies like RJM Technology and Axess Electronics. While his gear collection is certainly lust-worthy, all of the rigs have been assembled with the same basic signal routing and control, which makes it easy for John to move from rig to rig and not face the challenge of re-learning the complexity of operation.

With a recent South American G3 tour and the new, self-titled Dream Theater CD about to get backed up with a heavy dose of world touring, John felt it was time to go on a diet. No, not a hunger diet. A rig diet! He and his tech, Maddi Schieferstein, decided to pare things down to a compact rig that could deliver all the versatility, tone, and reliability that Petrucci requires, but in a fraction of the space. Reducing the complexity of the rig reduces the risk of problems and significantly reduces the cost of transportation.

The new touring rig hasn't been fully assembled yet, but what follows is a look at the rigs that John used on the G3 tour just prior to the recording of Dream Theater. His new touring rig will be a combination of the G3 touring rig plus some of what he used in the studio on the new record. Not pictured with John's latest rig photos is his new choice of MIDI foot controller: the RJM Music Technology MasterMind GT, which is now used in all of his rigs.

Fig. 11.10: G3 rig

John's latest G3 tour demonstrated the power of a compact rig. He switched back to using the Mesa/Boogie Triaxis preamp with the Mesa 2:Ninety stereo power amp, and he paired it with an Axe-FX II for most of his effects. A rackmounted Dunlop Cry Baby wah completed the setup. If you're not a Mesa/Boogie fanatic like me, you may not understand the relationship among John's favorite models of amplifier: the Triaxis is filled with the preamp circuits of classic Mark-series amps ranging from the Mark IIc+ through the Mark IV, and the Stereo Simul-Class 2:Ninety power amp is basically the power amp section of a Mark IV amp . . . times two! John's Mark V amps are mostly used for classic Mark-series tones, so there's no real "loss" of signature Petrucci tone whether he's playing a rig built around a Mark V, Mark IV, or Triaxis/2:Ninety.

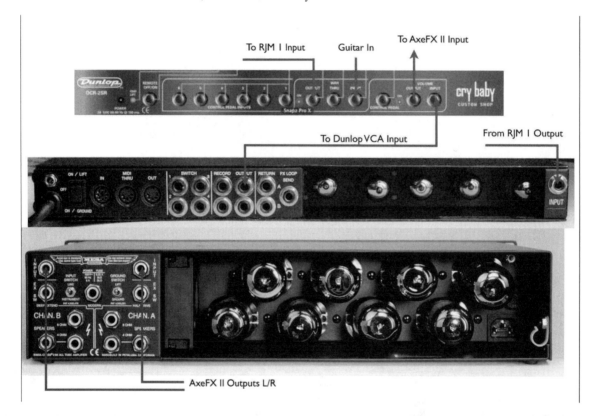

Fig. 11.11: Extremely straightforward connections for John's compact, G3 rig.

Next, here's a look at the Triaxis rig that Maddi and John assembled for use in the studio during the recording of Dream Theater. This gets a little closer to the live rig that is currently being assembled as this book goes to press. Multiple Triaxis preamps are installed for redundancy in case of a problem. With memory to store presets, there's no shortage of classic Mark-series tones instantly available from just a single preamp. Now if you're like me, you're probably super excited about the pedal trays in this next photo. You're looking at the Lowell RSD-116. I want it, but yikes! The all-steel shelf weighs sixteen pounds!

Fig. 11.12: Triaxis Rig

The following rig descriptions cover John's rigs up through the 2009/2010 tour supporting *Black Clouds & Silver Linings*.

Fig. 11.13: John Petrucci's Mark IV and Mark V "A" rigs are nearly identicaal

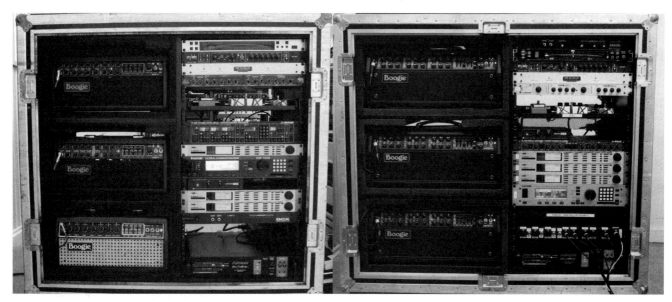

Fig. 11.14: All of John Petrucci's rigs are controlled via Axess Electronics FX1 MIDI foot controllers.

Things really aren't that complex in John's rigs, though. Everything about the design of his rigs is made for single-button simplicity. "Efficiency" is the word John used to describe the functional aspects of his equipment, right down to the logical design of his signature Music Man guitars. A three-position pickup selector provides a focused range of tones, and the guitars feature the most elegant implementation of piezo acoustic elements in any electric guitar (for more details, read the review at MusicPlayers.com).

While other pros rely on their switching systems to select between magnetic and piezo acoustic guitar outputs, the Music Man guitars enable John to switch from his acoustic tone to his Mark-series crunch in the span of an eighth note—an impossible feat on most other piezo-equipped guitars.

Each of John's rigs are controlled by the Axess Electronics FX1 MIDI Foot Controller. His friend Thomas Nordegg created some beautiful custom-colored stickers for the FX1's instant-access switches that match the appearance of the pedals tucked away on a rack shelf. Each pedalboard contains the same few items: a foot controller, volume pedal, wah pedal (actually a remote pedal interface for his rackmounted Dunlop Cry Baby), and a tuner. All the popular pedals are represented too. I found a BOSS TU-2, Korg Pitchblack, and TC Electronic polytune in the various rigs!

→ John's most recently used recording and touring rigs are built around the Mesa/Boogie Mark IV and Mark V, and he has rigs with either two or three heads in them (a primary "A" rig and a smaller "B" rig). While you might be quick to think he's running wet/dry/wet rigs, that's not the case. John prefers to avoid the complexity of wet/dry rigs and instead runs a basic stereo setup, with the third head providing access to additional preamp sounds if desired.

→ John's guitar cable (stereo) runs to a Framptone AB box. The piezo acoustic output goes to a Fishman Aura DI and then to the PA system. The magnetic output runs into the Cry Baby wah and finally into an Axess Electronics GRX4 looper, used for various front-of-amp pedal effects including an MXR EVH Phase 90 Phaser, MXR EVH Flanger, Ibanez Tube Screamer, a Mark L Vanilla Sky Overdrive, and a TC Electronic SCF Stereo Chorus Flanger (pedals vary from rig to rig, but usually include a few of these). A Voodoo Lab Pedal Power 2 Plus powers the effects.

→From the front-of-amp GRX4, the output goes into a Mesa/Boogie High Gain Amp Switcher. Part of this device's appeal is that it provides a shared effects loop for multiple devices, and the output from the HGAS feeds a second GRX4 for the effects loop portion of John's rig.

→Three of the GRX loops feed an Eventide DSP 7000 or 7600 harmonizer, TC Electronic 2290 delay, and TC Electronic M3000 reverb unit. The outputs from these effects go into a Digital Music Corp System Mix mixer and then to the effects returns of Amp A and Amp B.

→A TC Electronic 2290 or M3000 is constantly on, running a 7 ms delay to one side of the rig for spatial widening—i.e., big tone.

Fig. 11.15: Set them and forget them. A few pedals in John's rigs, easily swapped out when he wants to try something new for variety.

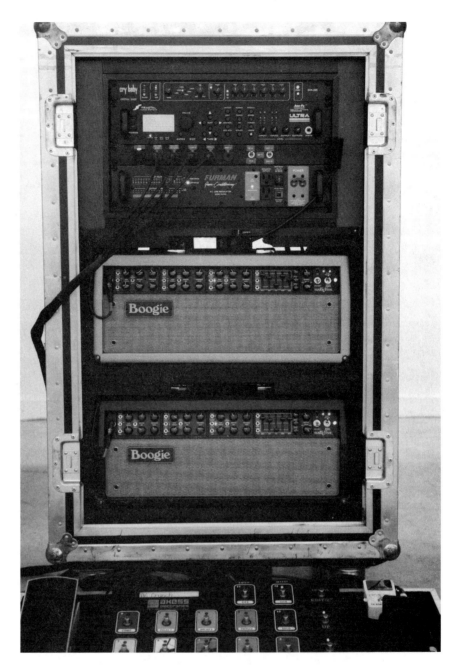

Fig. 11.16: John's most compact rig features an Axe-FX in place of all the pedals and rack effects seen in his big rigs.

Recently, John began using the Fractal Audio Axe-FX in his most compact-ever Mark V rig. As any touring musician knows, shipping your rig for fly-in gigs can be cost-prohibitive, and after being impressed by the quality of the effects programs in the Axe-FX, he set Mark Snyder to the task of building a compact stereo rig that eliminated the use of multiple rack effects processors and a tray full of pedals.

The signal path is extremely streamlined in this rig. Besides John's rackmounted Dunlop Cry Baby wah, which is the first device in the signal chain, the Axe-FX is connected via the popular four/five-cable scenario described earlier in the book so that some of its effects can be run in front of the amp's input and other effects can run in the effects loop.

The custom interface panel in the middle of the rig is essentially a custom pair of A/B switches, enabling John's guitar signal to run through the preamp section of one head and allowing the stereo returns from the Axe-FX to enter the effects loop returns on both heads for true stereo output.

Yes, the Axe-FX is capable of doing some great amp modeling, too. But as you can see from this rig, don't expect John to ditch his Mesa/Boogie tube amps any time soon.

Porcupine Tree: Steven Wilson and John Wesley

Builder: John Wesley

Listen to the incredible progressive rock band Porcupine Tree live and you'll hear fantastic, studio-rich guitar tones ranging from bone-crushing, dry metal tones to ethereal cleans with spacey effects to acoustic guitars and more. For a band you'd swear must use racks and racks of effects gear, the opposite is true: these guys keep it simple and keep it all on the floor.

Steven Wilson

Fig. 11.17: Steven Wilson's floor-based effects rig

As the lead singer and one of two guitarists in Porcupine Tree, Steven doesn't have time for a pedalboard tap dance when singing, so his rig is set up for instant gratification.

The signal path is straightforward: Guitar into a wah pedal into TheGigRig MIDI-8 controller. Steven's amp, a 50-watt Bad Cat head, The Lynx, has two independent channels and no effects loop. Two outputs run from the MIDI-8 to his amp: one for the clean channel and one for the dirty channel, enabling on-the-fly channel switching.

→ Steven gets effects from a TC Electronic G-System, which surprisingly runs in one of the loops in the MIDI-8.

→ Another loop in the MIDI-8 drives an Option 5 Destination Rotation Single effect pedal.

→ Connected to audio loops within the G-System are a few pedals: a Carl Martin Compressor, soundblox Multiwave Distortion, and a BOSS SD-2 Dual Overdrive.

→ Two BOSS FV-500H expression pedals are attached to the G-System for volume and expression control.

This somewhat unorthodox effects arrangement gives Steven the ability to instantly bypass the G-System (along with all of the pedals connected to it) via a single button press on the MIDI-8 when he plays his dry, heavy tones. Alternatively, stepping on the buttons in the G-System can change effects sounds without changing channels on the amp.

John Wesley

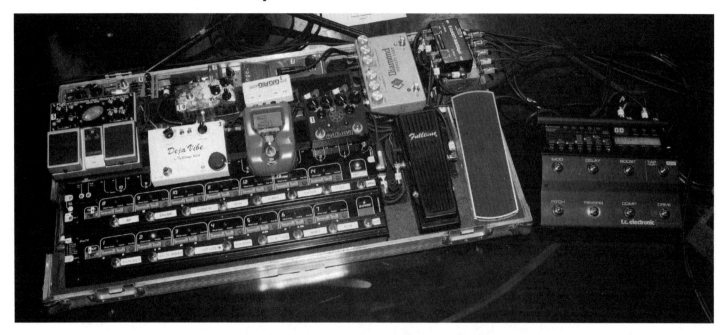

Fig. 11.18: John Wesley's floor-based effects rig

John Wesley, the famously unofficial fifth member of Porcupine Tree, tours with the band, playing guitars and singing, as well as contributing in various ways to their recordings. Outside of Porcupine Tree, John is also a fantastic prog rock solo artist with some great CDs, and his touring rig is also pretty easy to comprehend.

The pair of Marshall heads commonly seen behind John are late '70s Super Lead 100-watt heads custom-modded by amp guru Mark Cameron, but only one is ever in use at a time—the second is merely a backup in case of problems.

John's signal path is pretty straightforward, too: Guitar into a volume pedal into a Fulltone wah into TheGigRig Pro-14 controller. His Peterson tuner is always on, connected directly to a dedicated tuner output from the volume pedal. The output from the Pro-14 goes to the input on John's Marshall amp.

→ John runs a Diamond Memory Lane delay pedal and TC Electronic Nova System in the effects loop of his Marshall behind a compact looper, TheGigRig's Remote Loopy 2. The Marshall's loop Send goes into the Remote Loopy 2, and the output from the RL2 goes to the Marshall's Return. The RL2 has two audio loops, and each effect is run in one of them. A remote switch jack enables John to selectively enable either loop or bypass the effects completely, and this switch can be controlled from the Pro-14.

→ The piezo acoustic output from John's PRS guitar runs into TheGigRig's HumDinger, which provides a signal buffer and an isolated output to another amp (or in this case, the PA system). From there, the acoustic signal runs to a basic DI box, usually placed behind his amp.

→ The pedals in front of John's amp connect to individual loops within the Pro-14: Analog Man King of Tone, Fulltone Deja Vibe, BOSS RT-20 Rotary Ensemble, Analog Man Mini Chorus, Fulltone ChoralFlange, Klon Centaur, Vintage FX Colordrive, Dunlop '74 Vintage Phase 90, and Rockbox Boiling Point.

→ The bottom row of switches on John's Pro-14 provide instant access to specific presets that he has saved, but John also likes to mess with his pedals directly. The top row of switches on the Pro-14 provides instant access to his pedal loops.

→ A custom-built breakout box in the top right corner of the pedalboard provides easy connections for output to the amp, output from the guitar's piezo pickup, channel switching between two channels on his Marshall heads—controlled via the Pro-14, and Send and Return connections to the amp's effects loop. Physically, the output from the Pro-14 runs into the back of the breakout box, and then a cable connects between that jack and the amp.

Scott Kahn

Builder: Scott Kahn

Besides being the editor-in-chief of MusicPlayers.com, I'm also a professional guitar player. I was the founding guitarist for the progressive rock band Days Before Tomorrow, and in 2012 I moved on to launch my next band, aptly titled Beyond Tomorrow.

Hopefully by the time you read this book, Beyond Tomorrow will already be known to many of you, and of course if each of you purchases the band's debut CD in order to hear my latest guitar rig, that would go a long way toward fulfilling my dreams of rock 'n' roll stardom.

Like you and many of the players whose rigs I profiled, I have a rig that is constantly evolving. In fact, my 2010 rig—featured in the first edition of this book—has been replaced with a very different setup, and even that rig has evolved since I put it together in 2012.

First, I will talk about the 2010 rig, which was a fully rackmounted ENGL tube amp rig, and then I'll talk about the current rig, which is built around a traditional half-stack configuration with a separate effects rack and pedals.

Fig. 11.19: Scott's 2010 rig. All rackmounted tube gear and effects.

My 2010 rig was built around the ENGL e580 MIDI Tube Preamp and E850/100 stereo tube power amp. This combination packs an incredible array of ENGL's finest tones, from their famous studio-quiet clean tones to their tight, focused heavy tones, and an assortment of vintage, fuzz, and overdriven sounds in between. The preamp's effects loop is both parallel and series (when set to 100 percent wet), and the beauty of having separate preamp and power amp units is how easily you can place different items in the signal chain. In my rig, I had a few pedals in front of the preamp (hidden behind the two-space rack panel and connected to loops in the RJM Music Technology RG-16) and a TC Electronic G-System in the effects loop.

The guitar signal came in via a Shure SLX wireless system, which runs into the rear of the preamp. If I needed to, I could plug a guitar cable into the front of the preamp, which automatically bypasses the wireless system as the front input jack takes priority over the one in the rear of the unit.

An RJM Music Technology RG-16 was used to provide function switching for changing a few settings on the 850/100. The power amp has two alternate volume levels, and different Presence and Depth settings that are each switchable, and thus I could control them via the RG-16.

A TC Electronic G-System Limited was wired to provide effects both in front of the amp and in the effects loop via a five-cable hookup (this is a stereo rig), and its foot controller controlled the ENGL e580 preamp as well as the RG-16. This was a straightforward system that sounded huge.

In a live setting, the rig ran through an ENGL Pro–series 4×12 cabinet in stereo. But for recording, rather than returning the G-System effects to the effects loop return, I ran the output into a Peavey Classic Series 50/50 stereo tube power amp and into a Mesa/Boogie 2×12 speaker cabinet wired in stereo, instantly transforming the rig into a wet/dry/wet rig. But without a team of roadies, the wet/dry/wet rig was strictly for the studio.

In 2012, I fell in love all over again, this time with the ENGL Powerball II head, which had a very different personality tone-wise from the e580/850 setup. I changed my life for her, and thus began the next period of creativity and inspiration.

Fig. 11.20: Scott's 2012–13 guitar rig.

For the 2012 rig, I needed to build a small rack just for my effects, and I didn't need a shock-mounted case since there would be no tube gear in the rack. I opted for a 10U rack from Calzone Case Company that utilized their XLT composite material instead of traditional plywood. It provides all the strength of a wooden rack but at 25 percent of the weight of ¼-inch plywood. And another benefit to the composite material: you can Velcro things like your line mixer to the inside of the case (which doesn't always work so well on unfinished plywood).

I needed more instant access foot switches than the G-System provided, so I replaced my G-System with the TC Electronic G-Major 2 and paired it with a Mark L FC-25 MIDI foot controller. The G-Major 2 has the same sound engine as the G-System, so I didn't have to sacrifice my sounds to make this change.

My upgrades didn't stop there—this was one costly love affair! It was time to make the switch to digital wireless, and the Line 6 Relay G90 replaced my Shure SLX analog system.

Holding all the pieces together used to be an RJM Music Technology RG-16, but I replaced it with the newer Rack Gizmo. Did it really make a difference in my rig? Not much, but I felt that I owed it to the readers of this book to keep up with the latest technology. At least, that's how I justified the purchase to myself.

Fig. 11.21: Scott's 2013 rig diagram, almost . . .

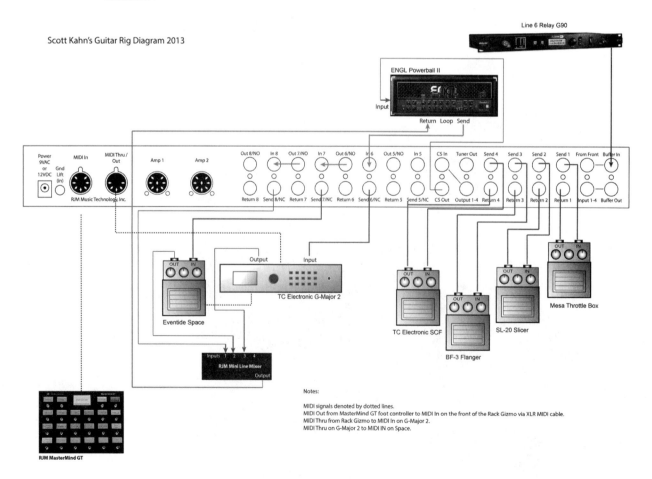

I also incorporated a few more pedals into the rig, now residing on a slide-out SKB pedal shelf, and added the RJM Mini Line Mixer in the back of the rig so that my Eventide Space pedal and TC Electronic G-Major 2 (which both lived in my effects loop) could be bypassed without cutting off any reverb tails and delay repeats.

Most recently (summer 2013), I replaced the FC-25 foot controller with the RJM Technology MasterMind GT, and I replaced the rack with a larger shock-mounted SKB case (pictured below) so that I have more room for neat and tidy cabling as well as easier access to my pedal shelf, which is seeing more action than ever before as I explore some new textures as well as overdrives.

Fig. 11.22: Scott's 2013-14 guitar rig

CHAPTER 12

Interviews with Rig Builders

I spoke with multiple rig builders while working on this book to find out about their approaches to rig design and their thoughts on the specific aspects of rig design that are of concern to all professional guitarists.

This chapter opens with my conversation with legendary guitar systems builder Bob Bradshaw, president of Custom Audio Electronics. He *is* the rig man. Without his pioneering rig-building work, I wouldn't have had very much to talk about in this book. He is the godfather of modern-day guitar rigs.

Bob Bradshaw

Custom Audio Electronics
www.customaudioelectronics.com

Clients: Steve Lukather, Michael Landau, Eddie Van Halen, David Gilmour, Eric Clapton, Peter Frampton, Andy Summers, Steve Vai, Warren Haynes, John Mayer, The Edge

When you design a new rig for a musician, what are some of the questions you like to address up front for designing a proper rig?

Basically, what are you using now? What are you trying to achieve? As in, is this a live rig where you need to re-create prerecorded music? Or is this a studio rig where you would have more time to craft sounds? These things matter when deciding on specific pieces of gear to use in the system. Also, where do you see the rig going in the future? Space must be allotted for future expansion if necessary.

What do you consider the most important design considerations for a touring guitar rig?

Reliability and ease of use. And as simple a signal path as possible while being able to cover all bases musically.

Are there some common features that most musicians ask you to incorporate into their rigs, and do you have standard gear that you use to implement those requests?

Well, my situation is a bit unique, as I design and manufacture the equipment I use in the design of my systems. Most rig builders must rely on prebuilt off-the-shelf products in their systems. There are exceptions to this of course, but not many. That said, my designs are wide open in terms of signal path (audio routing). I can create a unique signal path for each player's needs. Pretty much anything goes here within reason.

But all systems utilize my RS MIDI foot controllers (RS-10, RS-5, or the new RS-T), which could be considered "standard." These foot controllers offer what I refer to as the "Direct Access" approach: that is, there is a dedicated footswitch (and LED indicator) for every switchable function in the system, in addition to separate "preset" switches to allow for combinations of the Direct Access controllers as well as MIDI program change commands. Direct Access means you don't have to rely on presets for your sounds, and you can edit on the fly, like you would with a traditional pedalboard with individual effects.

But basically, people come to me for a clean, transparent signal path, and I try my best to make it sound as close to plugging straight into the amp as possible. When everything is bypassed, of course!

What are some of the more unique/custom requests that some artists have requested in their rigs?

I consider *all* of my systems unique, because everyone's needs are different; therefore, they all use different stuff, which keeps it fun and interesting after over thirty years of doing this. I always try to stick to the signal path the client is used to, no matter how "wrong" it may seem, because I feel anything goes.

Experimenting is the only way to find new sounds. So I always ask what signal path order the client has been using. It got a bit "cookie cutter" in the late '80s, as people would just come to me and have me put stuff in any order I wanted, with little input from the player. But I always prefer to collaborate with the "driver" of the rig.

I suppose an early rig that was interesting was one I did for Warren Cuccurullo that utilized a Yamaha mixer with moving faders . . . it was quite involved for that era. Warren created some amazing soundscapes on his *Machine Language* record with that rig. He even named it Delilah.

Another was a live looping rig I built for Andy Summers, based on Eventide harmonizers. This was prior to all the great (and easy to use) looping devices available now. Andy did a solo tour opening for Tangerine Dream with this rig. And I mean solo—just him and the rig onstage. Very brave!

And Greg Edwards of Autolux has quite a unique setup/signal path. He uses his boxes in quite an unconventional order to achieve his unique sounds. And let's not forget The Edge—a true sonic adventurer. The rigs I have designed and built for him are interesting in their sheer size and scope. The signal path is relatively simple: a mono chain out to multiple amps, but there is a lot of gear involved, as he likes to use whatever was used to make the records, with little compromise. So as the years go by and the set list gets longer, so does the signal path!

What value do you find in using a line mixer in a complex guitar rig? Do all rigs that you build need them?

Well, I pioneered the use of line mixers (and designed and manufactured my own) over twenty-five years ago to solve a basic problem I was having using multiple effects processors in stereo guitar rigs. In the early days, most "stereo" devices were mono in/stereo out. And even if they had two input jacks, they were rarely true stereo all the way through the box. The input signal was often summed to mono, then processed into "pseudo stereo," then spit out. Therefore, your stereo imaging gets jumbled up when trying to connect multiple effects boxes in a series chain, one after the other.

Remember too, this was before multi-effects boxes that could solve this problem internally. But to me, I never cared for most multi-effects anyway, as there were too many sonic compromises made to jam a ton of effects into one box. That's why many of my rigs were so large: multiple individual effects boxes.

Anyway, another problem was passing your "dry" unprocessed signal through so many boxes, hoping they were nice to your signal. Usually they were not. So I developed a stereo "line mixer" that 1) passed your dry, unprocessed signal through a minimum of circuitry, thus maintaining its sonic integrity; and 2) allowed the use of multiple stereo devices to be used in true stereo by putting them in parallel.

My line mixers are dual/stereo, as there are two stereo mixers in one box, in series with each other to allow for some series effects processing, which is often necessary. Another benefit of line mixers in my systems was the ability of the time-based effect to "trail" off naturally when bypassed, because all you had to do was mute the input signal to the effect.

Not all rigs need mixers. They are best suited for time-based effects such as reverb, chorus, and delay. And the effect needs to be able to be set 100 percent wet (with separate output level adjustment) because you are now mixing your effect with your dry, unprocessed signal, which passes through the mixer separately. Not all effects boxes (especially pedals) can do this. Also, there are many instances when you need to effect your signal 100 percent, and that is not always easy to do with a line mixer, unless you have a switching system or a way to mute your dry signal while allowing only the effect to pass through.

What's your preference for custom cabling?

I use Mogami cable pretty much exclusively for audio signals: #2524 for most unbalanced long runs and #2319 for pedalboards, due to its smaller diameter. I have tried pretty much everything, and I prefer Mogami for its sonic quality and ease of use. I use a combination of Neutrik, Amphenol, and Switchcraft connectors, always soldered.

How have custom rigs changed or evolved over the years since you started building them? Have you seen any particular trends in terms of what players used to want vs. what they want today?

When I started out, it was pretty much all pedals, as there were very few "rack" effects available, as this was considered "professional" studio gear. But studio players were the guys I catered to at first, and they started bringing me studio effects processors to be integrated into their guitar rigs, along with their pedals. This is where I learned to interface gear properly. Dealing with impedance, buffering, line vs. instrument levels, etc. So the integration of rackmounted processors along with pedals in terms of effects was an evolutionary process, along with changes in amplifier technology such as amp heads vs. rackmounted preamp/power amp configurations.

Way back when, there were no "effects loops" in amps. All effects had to come between the instrument output and the amplifier input. But I wanted the sound of a miked amp with effects *after* the amp sound, like I heard on records. So I took an amp head, replaced the speaker with a load device, padded that output signal down to line level, then processed this signal with effects and sent the signal to power amps. Since I already had the whole sound of the original amp, I didn't need tone here, just power to push the speakers. Instant "post effects" sound! And no amp effects loop needed.

Eventually, I went back to the speaker instead of the load device on the "tone" amp, and the wet/dry configuration was born. I developed an amp selector that would allow switching between up to four amps in the same common cabinet (or load device) to accommodate players needing many different amp sounds. Individual line outs were provided to drive the effects/power amps. An offshoot of this was the component approach; that is, a multichannel guitar preamp and separate power amps to drive the speakers. By placing effects between the preamp output/power amp inputs, you have an instant "effects loop" with complete isolation between front-end gain/tone stages and the power stage of a guitar amplification system. The merits of this are debatable, as with any configuration, and I have always maintained that a good preamp/guitar amp-voiced power amp combination is as good as, if not better than, any amp head, especially when it comes to integrating effects into the equation.

[As for trends,] it's all back to pedals to a large extent these days. There was quite an evolution in technology back in the '80s, as rackmounted effects came to the forefront. Pedals took a bit of a back seat there for a while. But manufacturers started packing too much mediocre stuff into one box, which resulted in the "multi-effect." Some were good, and some were bad. And I think guitar players tired of having to scroll through "presets" and "menus" to find a sound. I know I did! As a result, racks and "rackmounted" effects got a bad rap over time.

Most guitar players want instant gratification, and pedals give you that. Plus they are lighter, cheaper, and with pedals, you are not putting all your eggs in one basket as you would with a multi-effect. Your pedalboard becomes your "basket." But as with anything, there is good and bad with both. There sure are a lot of crappy pedals out there, too! So I do a lot of interfacing of both, just like I did when I started, over thirty years ago.

Also, people are more aware of what a good switching/looping system can do for your rig. It cleans up your signal path tremendously and can be a great benefit, even in the smallest of configurations. Not to mention being able to control everything from a MIDI foot controller. To that end, I have developed what I call a pedalboard switching system, or PSS. It consists of a pedalboard-mounted audio router/controller, and when connected to the new RS-T MIDI foot controller, it offers a pedalboard-based system with all the power of a rackmounted rig. With the advent of new MIDI-controlled pedals, everything can be "onboard." Just connect guitar and amps.

Do you have any advice for dealing with the different power requirements and wireless regulations for internationally touring artists?

Power conditioning is important, and a good power regulator that maintains a constant mains voltage is a good investment. To me, wireless is a showbiz necessity, a necessary evil. In my opinion, you can't make a cable out of air. But many try, and again, some are better than others, with the better ones costing thousands of dollars. I applaud those artists who refuse to use them.

Everything I do to maintain sonic purity integrating passive guitars/effects/amps gets thrown out the window when wireless systems come into the mix. That said, I often build "source selectors" of various sizes to accommodate multiple wireless transmitter/receiver combinations. This requires careful consideration when interfacing, as wireless comes first in the signal path pre gain, and being active, can contribute quite a bit of noise if not treated with respect.

How do you typically price the building of a custom rig?

As you would expect, the bigger the system, the more costly. My custom systems are priced on a per switchable function basis. The RS foot controllers are a fixed price, but expandable to accommodate the custom switching functions. Therefore, more switchable functions equals more money.

I charge an hourly rate, but I am pretty flexible when it comes to pricing, and I always try to work within a budget. I often end up shooting myself in the foot here, though! I always try to add a little more in terms of features, etc., that I don't ultimately charge for. People have to remember that my systems are labor intensive; they are not necessarily "off the shelf" products, and the ones that could fall into that category are limited-production items and most are actually built by me. Custom systems can be either rack- or pedalboard-based or a combination of both. And initial consultations are free!

David Phillips and Martin Golub

L.A. Sound Design
www.lasounddesign.net
info@lasounddesign.net

Clients: 311, Green Day, Tom Petty & the Heartbreakers, REO Speedwagon, Snow Patrol, Goo-Goo Dolls, Mötley Crüe, Michael Landau, Paul Jackson Jr., Tim Pierce

When you design a new rig for a musician, what are some of the questions you like to address up front for designing a proper rig?

What equipment are they using? What type of tone are they going for? Who are their influences?

What do you consider the most important design considerations for a touring guitar rig?

The quality of parts and durability.

Are there some common features that most musicians ask you to incorporate into their rigs, and do you have standard gear that you use to implement those requests?

Some common features asked for are A/B switching between amps, loop boxes, custom buffers, etc. We make everything custom for the particular rig we are doing.

What are some of the more unique/custom requests that some artists have requested in their rigs?

One request was to be able to switch eight amps on and off with dual MIDI controllers.

What value do you find in using a line mixer in a complex guitar rig? Do all rigs that you build need them?

They help keep the noise down and the dry signal more pure by running the effects in parallel. We use them in elaborate W/D/W systems and on some pedalboards with digital delays.

What's your preference for custom cabling?

We use Mogami, Belden, and Switchcraft.

How have custom rigs changed or evolved over the years since you started building them? Have you seen any particular trends in terms of what players used to want vs. what they want today?

Better, more compact hardware is available (RJM Music Technology, Musicom Lab). There has been a resurgence of players using pedalboards because of the ease of setup and ability to travel. Also, MIDI loop switchers have become very popular.

Do you have any advice for dealing with the different power

requirements and wireless regulations for internationally touring artists?

You can travel with a step transformer or use multiple power supplies for wherever you are traveling. The Burkey Flatliner is one of the best power supplies [for effects pedals] because of its versatility, and it can run at 120V and 220V. As far as wireless units go, the Line 6 units are perfect for the US and international use. They are some of the best on the market.

How do you typically price the building of a custom rig?

Our pedalboards are based on a price that includes the labor, board, power supply and interface for a certain amount of pedals. Racks are quoted per job and include labor and parts and any custom hardware required.

Mark Snyder

FramptoneMS@aol.com

Clients: John Petrucci, Peter Frampton, Alex Lifeson, Vernon Reid

When you design a new rig for a musician, what are some of the questions you like to address up front for designing a proper rig?

I like to get a sense of what the player's requirements are: number and types of sounds, number and types of effects, front end and back end. Overall sonic goal—sound quality vs. convenience vs. reliability.

What do you consider the most important design considerations for a touring guitar rig?

Reliability. It is crucial that a rig be reliable day in and day out, all over the world. I am also fond of building in "worst-case scenario" solutions, such as, What if the amp or foot controller dies mid-show, and how can that be overcome on the fly?

Are there some common features that most musicians ask you to incorporate into their rigs, and do you have standard gear that you use to implement those requests?

Guitar switching is a common one. I have designed a very simple guitar switcher that allows the tech to seamlessly execute guitar changes, or mute the guitar signal at the end of show. Almost all the rigs I have built involve the use of multiple amps, which usually creates a grounding, phase, or high-noise situation. I designed the Framptone Amp Switcher to address those issues, and I have been able to create more elaborate setups utilizing the Amp Switcher principles and technology.

What are some of the more unique/custom requests that some artists have requested in their rigs?

In one of John's older rigs, when I was still touring with DT as his tech, we realized that the pickup output of his Ernie Ball guitar was so hot that even the most conservative input gain settings on his MK IVs would still clip in the clean mode. John's clean sound is very crucial, and the only way we were able to get the amp setting "clean" again was to turn down his guitar volume slightly. I recalled running into this same problem years earlier with Jazz legend Pat Martino. Pat was not willing to slightly turn down his guitar volume, so in the end, I built a custom box for him that was basically an inline guitar volume, reversed in polarity, so that at "zero" there was no effect at all, but as you turned it up, the guitar "cleaned up." He thought I was brilliant, even though as you turned up the box, it was basically like turning down the guitar. John and I laughed about it, and I built a similar box for John's rig, which we named the PMB1 (Pat Martino Box). We put it in a loop that was programmable before the entire rig so that it could be easily programmed on the clean sounds . . . quite an elaborate method of turning down the guitar "slightly"!

What value do you find in using a line mixer in a complex guitar rig? Do all rigs that you build need them?

I do like mixers in most rigs, but I did not always think that way. I have always strived for the simplest and most direct method of achieving all the sounds wanted, while preserving the purity of the tone. I have always thought to myself, "The mixing transformer in a $3,000 effect unit must be sonically better than the six mixing transformers in this $300 mixer unit!" That being said, the way the effects interact is completely different in a parallel system. I actually prefer mixers that do not have individual volume controls . . . just more to get into the signal path. I really like the one that Bob made, and the one that Digital Music used to make. I would always modify them, because I like when there is a single "dry" input with a level control, and another single level control for all the effects. You control the level of each effect with the individual effect's level controls.

What's your preference for custom cabling?

I like Mogami wire and Neutrik connectors. I only use solder connectors. I have also had some great results with the Planet Waves cables from a sonic perspective. I have done several "blind" cable shootouts, and Mogami and Planet Waves always came out on top. I have very specific goals for cables. Their sonic "job" is very important. Their job is to do *nothing*. I have found several cables that offer lots of enhancement, but that is not what I am looking for. A cable should do its job . . . nothing.

How have custom rigs changed or evolved over the years since you started building them? Have you seen any particular trends in terms of what players used to want vs. what they want today?

I have seen a few interesting trends, but I do not find them universal with the rig community. Just when I think "big rigs are out," someone contacts me to build a monster rig! I think people do want more flexibility in a smaller package, but I am always very conservative in my thinking. I like to use the best units for the job, and I am skeptical about "all in one" units and amps. The Fractal unit might just change my mind, however. Pedals seemed to be the wave of the future . . . again, but I am starting to see that slip, and people are going back to multiple amps! I think there will always be a diverse rig community, and it will always be cyclical. Just think—records are coming back. Who would have predicted that?

Do you have any advice for dealing with the different power requirements and wireless regulations for internationally touring artists?

I am not a fan of guitar wireless. I forced many guitarists, including John and Peter, back to the "leash"! To me, there is some strange, difficult to describe "connection" you get when you plug in vs. a wireless. In terms of power, I think it is a highly overlooked aspect of rig sound quality and reliability. I always check power before firing up rigs, and if there is some strange phase reversal, grounding issue, or voltage leakage, I resolve it before even plugging the rig in.

How do you typically price the building of a custom rig?

I have always tried to price rig work fairly. I charge based on the time it takes to build and program the rig. If there are technical obstacles, I view that as my responsibility, and I do not generally charge the client for working through those obstacles. I simply make sure that my trusty rig-building accomplice, Mike Buffa, is compensated for his time, and that material costs are covered. The complex and difficult projects are the most fun, so I would certainly not charge more for them!

David Friedman

Tone Merchants & Rack Systems
www.tonemerchants.com

Clients: Eddie Van Halen, Steve Stevens, The Offspring, Bon Jovi, My Chemical Romance, Alice in Chains

When you design a new rig for a musician, what are some of the questions you like to address up front for designing a proper rig?

Really, I ask them what they need to get out of the rig and what are some of the things they want, or would like, to use. Or, if they need guidance, I provide it where needed.

What do you consider the most important design considerations for a touring guitar rig?

To make it easy and functional and, of course, bulletproof. Also, make a rig that can be added to if needed down the road.

Are there some common features that most musicians ask you to incorporate into their rigs, and do you have standard gear that you use to implement those requests?

Well, mostly to have the ability to program combinations of effects and amps at the click of one switch. Also to have their tech have the ability to switch the rig also. I use many different products to accomplish this. One brand is not good for everything.

What are some of the more unique/custom requests that some artists have requested in their rigs?

Some artists have asked to do strange signal paths and amp combinations. Others have wanted very elaborate rigs. Some have been for guitar players or the odd violinist. I find violin through a whammy and some distortion a lot of fun, and there was a sax pedalboard or two.

What value do you find in using a line mixer in a complex guitar rig? Do all rigs that you build need them?

Line mixers are only needed when the artist is using a processor at line level and wants to maintain a dry, unaffected path. This is so it won't color the tone or have unneeded latency.

What's your preference for custom cabling?

Mogami 2319 cable mostly, but we do use others on request. As far as ends—Switchcraft and/or Neutrik.

How have custom rigs changed or evolved over the years since you started building them? Have you seen any particular trends in terms of what players used to want vs. what they want today?

In the '80s and early '90s most rigs were made up of rackmounted processors and preamps and/or amps. Not too many pedals were happening then. Later in the '90s racks kind of went away for pedalboards, and now it's sort of a mix of both.

Do you have any advice for dealing with the different power requirements and wireless regulations for internationally touring artists?

Well, most of the rigs are done at 117V. When a band goes abroad the power requirements are taken care of by the production. It's hard to do rigs that switch voltages sometimes, so it is better to stay with one. As far as wireless, most are up to date now, and that is what is generally used.

How do you typically price the building of a custom rig?

Rigs are priced via an hourly rate. After years of doing this I sort of know how many hours things are going to take. So it's that, plus all parts and/or equipment purchased.

Scott Appleton

PHI Electronics
www.scottappleton.com
Clients: Alex Lifeson, Neal Schon, Phil Collen

When you design a new rig for a musician, what are some of the questions you like to address up front for designing a proper rig?

Most artists have a really good idea of what they would like to accomplish in their heads, so the first things to find out are what gear they prefer to use, and any specific signal routing that they have in mind. Most of the time an artist has an existing rig that needs to be modified to suit his current needs, but occasionally you need to start from the ground up.

What do you consider the most important design considerations for a touring guitar rig?

Durability/dependability. If the artist's gear doesn't work gig after gig, you won't either.

Are there some common features that most musicians ask you to incorporate into their rigs, and do you have standard gear that you use to implement those requests?

Most of the artists I have worked with each have their own approach. The key is to figure out how *they* work, and then how to fulfill those needs. What works for Alex Lifeson will not work for Neal Schon, and vice versa. As far as gear, there are certain pieces that I will tend to use, because I know they are reliable and will accomplish what the artist requires.

What are some of the more unique/custom requests that some artists have requested in their rigs?

I have used gear for purposes they weren't originally intended for. For example, in Alex Lifeson's rig, we use a Fishman Aura for the piezo output of his PowerBridge-equipped Les Pauls. The Aura is intended to be used with acoustic instruments, but works very well with the PowerBridge system. I have had clients who refused to use any transformers in the signal path—that created some unique challenges, particularly when splitting the signal to several amplifiers.

What value do you find in using a line mixer in a complex guitar rig? Do all rigs that you build need them?

Not every rig requires them, but I do find more times than not that they are needed in a large rig situation. In my opinion, there really is no other option if the artist prefers to use multiple dedicated effects processors to achieve their tone.

What's your preference for custom cabling?

I like Mogami and George L's; however, I always use soldered ends. Generally I will only use George L's inside a rack or on a pedalboard—not for a snake.

How have custom rigs changed or evolved over the years since you started building them? Have you seen any particular trends in terms of what players used to want vs. what they want today?

I built my first racks in the days when everything was rackmounted, and went through the rack backlash, seeing most players revert to an amp and pedals. With the artists I work with, I tend to see a hybrid of both these days. Most are using their favorite amps, and the pedals are on a shelf in a rack with a switcher and a couple of rackmounted effects. Best of all worlds.

Do you have any advice for dealing with the different power requirements and wireless regulations for internationally touring artists?

As for power, I use the Furman AR-Pro when possible. It can take pretty much anything you can throw at it voltage wise. As for wireless, that can be a bit of a challenge. With digital television invading our airwaves, and the sale of the 700 MHz frequency bands this year, all you can really do is get the best frequency-agile wireless the artist can afford, and replace wireless units that are now rendered "illegal." As for touring in foreign countries, you do need to be aware of local laws regarding wireless usage, but a high-quality unit should get you by in almost any situation.

How do you typically price the building of a custom rig?

Typically I just charge a flat rate based on the complexity of the rig.

CHAPTER 13

Putting It All Together: Building Your Rig

Hopefully this book has filled your head with all sorts of new ideas related to building pro guitar rigs. There are tons of great products out there to enable you to make your rig do whatever you can dream up, and if you reach out to the manufacturers, they're typically very helpful when it comes to putting their products to use. But if you're at the point where you've got a few amps and some effects, you might be wondering where to begin in taking your rig to the next level. Here are some thoughts regarding what comes next. Yes, this is effectively the chapter where I tell you where to go.

Your Amplifier

The place to start begins with your amp, since ultimately, this is the heart and soul of your tone engine. Your fingers are what give life to your style, and your guitar translates your style into energy, but the amp ultimately has the greatest influence on your actual sound. No matter how you hit the strings on your Strat going into a Fender Twin, it's not going to sound like playing a Jackson Soloist into a Mesa/Boogie Dual Rectifier, though the style and vibe of your playing may still make you identifiable to the listener.

If you've been thinking about getting a new amp, like so many other decisions in life it's all about getting the right tool for the job. And if your job calls for a Diamond Nitrox, no matter how much you love the Vox AC-15, the latter is not going to be the right tool for the job.

Players in cover bands or those seeking a wide variety of tones should definitely consider some of the programmable rackmounted guitar amps and preamps. Many traditional amps are capable of delivering a wide range of tones, but if you only have access to two or three channels, you can't really take advantage of all of those tones in the live setting.

Still love the idea of a head on top of your cabinet? Check out amps from ENGL, Hughes & Kettner, and others who offer MIDI control over their amps with memory for multiple presets beyond the few channels on the face of the amp. But note that just because an amp has MIDI control doesn't automatically mean it has memory for multiple presets. For example, the Marshall JVM series has great MIDI functionality, but the controls just switch between the two or four channels on the head and the various settings for reverb and effects loops. By comparison, the ENGL Special Edition E670 head has physical controls for a few channels as well as memory for saving up to 128 different presets. The Hughes & Kettner Coreblade has presets and onboard effects too!

Trying to create a unique sound that nobody else has? Rack gear lets you mix and match preamps with power amps—something you can't really do otherwise. And if you like the idea of building a stereo or wet/dry rig, there's no easier way.

Effects

Clean up your effects chain. If you're still stringing pedals together in series, it's time to get an audio looper. You can keep your pedals on the floor if you like to twist knobs, but you might also want to consider sticking your pedals on a shelf in a small rack and adding a rackmounted audio looper and a MIDI foot controller to change your pedal selections. Obviously you'll need a power source for your pedals, and although we didn't discuss those in this book, I'm willing to bet that some of you are still sticking 9V batteries in your pedals. Numerous power options are available for your pedals, and the same options for powering a pedalboard work in a rack too.

Another advantage of audio loopers is that they make it easy for you to place some of your effects in your effects loop and keep some effects in front of your amp; also, putting your pedals in a rack allows you to have short cable runs between your effects and your amp for the highest sound quality.

Consider a rackmounted multi-effects processor to eliminate a few pedals from your collection. You can get studio-quality effects that sound incredible for the price of just a few good pedals, and products like the G-Major 2 are extremely easy to use.

Effects Loop Considerations

Do you want to buy old gear from the '80s and '90s on eBay, or do you want to play with newer gear? If you embrace vintage effects, make sure your amp has a parallel effects loop. Running your entire signal through an effects device that lacks true bypass or has old A/D converters will compromise your tone. If your amp has a series loop, all you need is a small line mixer, which will enable you to convert the series loop to a parallel loop.

If you plan to put multiple effects units in your parallel loop but want to run them in series, you might want to invest in a line mixer for this application too, but make sure you get a mixer that gives you individual level control over the devices connected to it. Otherwise, you might have a hard time balancing the levels of your digital delay unit and your chorus pedal, for example.

If you're using modern rack gear like the G-Series, Eclipse, or Axe-FX, a series loop is fine, since the A/D converters in these units are state of the art. But research your effects gear first! There are many products on the market, like the G-Force, that have been around for years and don't have the latest A/D converters. These products sound great, but you'll want to put them in a parallel loop for the highest-quality results.

MIDI Foot Controllers

By now you understand the advantages of MIDI foot controllers for controlling your rig. There are numerous controllers on the market, and while this book highlighted many of the larger, professional models, virtually every company whose products I talked about also offers smaller, more affordable foot controllers that may do everything you need. For example, if you're using an RJM RG-16 to control your amp functions and put a bunch of your pedals in audio loops, the compact Mastermind foot controller is all you need to change sounds.

Rack Case Planning

It's a good idea to consider what kind of a rig you're building before buying or ordering a rack case. Make a list of all the items you're thinking of placing in the rack so you can figure out how many spaces you'll need to accommodate all the gear.

A simple rack containing a power conditioner (1U), wireless receiver (1U), and multi-effects processor (1U) requires three rack spaces. A rack containing a power conditioner (1U), wireless system (1U), shelf with pedals (2 or 3U), and audio looper (1U) will require five or six spaces. Building a system with a preamp usually adds two spaces, and a power amp can add between two and five spaces, depending on its size—and then you should leave at least one or two spaces open in the rack above the power amp for air circulation and cooling.

Want to add a drawer? As you can see, racks can grow big pretty easily. Plus, you always want to leave a few extra spaces open for future expansion. Buying a new rack just to accommodate a single extra device is a costly and time-consuming proposition.

If you're handling the gear personally and it's just an effects rig (no tube amps), there's no need to spend money on a shock rack. Besides costing significantly more, they weigh more than twice as much as standard racks and are significantly bulkier, which can be a big issue if you're moving the gear personally in your car. SKB's standard cases are lightweight and compact—perfect for the effects rack that is used primarily for local transport. And there are plenty of rugged plywood rack cases available without shock systems, too. Just be careful with them in the back of your car. With their metal corners and solid mass, I've heard of more than a few people blowing out the rear window of a hatchback or SUV when they hit a bump and their rack was close to the window, especially if the casters underneath the rack weren't in their locked position.

Wireless Nirvana

Finally a word to the wireless. Buy rechargeable batteries! They're better for the environment, tend to last longer than typical alkalines, and save you a ton of money. When you buy your rechargeable batteries, take a permanent marker and label them in pairs so you never mix and match batteries of different ages, which will result in a much shorter battery life.

Gratuitous Plug

Be sure to visit www.MusicPlayers.com to read in-depth reviews of pro gear like that featured in this book, plus guitars, amps, recording equipment, and more. We also feature great tutorials and artist interviews with players who have larger rigs than you do.

Have questions about using all this gear in your new rig? There's an MGR forum at MusicPlayers.com where I will answer all questions about building your guitar rig.

And if you're a fan of melodic progressive rock music, check out my band, Beyond Tomorrow, at the following locations online:

Website: www.beyondtomorrowband.com
Facebook: www.facebook.com/beyondtomorrowband
Reverb Nation: www.reverbnation.com/beyondtomorrowband

CHAPTER 14

Making the Switch to In-Ear Monitoring

Although not necessarily part of your guitar rig, in-ear monitors provide the safest way to listen to your guitar rig when performing live. If you're running around on stage with a wireless instrument system, IEMs (as they are called) ensure that you'll never be chained to one fixed position on stage again. Here's everything you need to know about in-ear monitoring and personal monitoring systems to get you started.

In-Ear Monitoring 101

I love playing live, but there are times when the monitoring in a club is so bad that you don't get to hear things nearly as well as when you're in the comfort of your band's rehearsal studio. And who doesn't enjoy a blissful stereo headphone mix in the recording studio? Bad monitoring can kill the vibe of any performance, and if the vocalists in your band can't hear themselves and each other clearly, you can bet that off-pitch vocals will destroy the sound of your live performance.

Unless you live under a rock—like those cavemen in the television commercial—you know that thousands of professional musicians rely upon in-ear monitoring, and for good reason: in-ear monitors can deliver studio-quality sound for stage monitoring at a safe listening level. If your band struggles to nail vocal parts because you can't hear each other well enough, in-ears will make a huge difference. Can't hear your guitar loudly enough over the other guys in the band to execute your scariest shred licks with surgical precision? In-ears will help. Can't hear the syncopated electronic drum loop or click track your band requires from behind your kit? Again, in-ears will take you places that floor wedges or traditional headphones never dared to tread. And, they'll protect your hearing in the process.

Everyone from Lady Gaga to Metallica to Dream Theater uses in-ear monitors today, and even if you're just playing at the club level or rehearsing in an hourly studio rental, you can put this technology to use. No matter what genre of music you play, IEM technology can radically improve both the quality of your musical performance and your enjoyment of the sound of your band in a live venue.

Getting started with in-ear monitoring can seem confusing because it requires understanding a few different pieces of the puzzle and learning how they fit together. Since companies advertise individual parts of the puzzle, many newcomers to the in-ear monitoring world find themselves unsure of exactly where to begin.

In this tutorial, we've laid out those puzzle pieces in order to help you put the right picture together. Here's what you'll need to understand in order to put this essential technology to use:

→ In-ear monitors (IEMs), the actual ear buds/speakers used for monitoring audio.

→ Personal monitoring systems (PMS), the wireless transmitter and receiver than send a monitor mix from the mixing board to your IEMs.

→ Integrating the personal monitoring system with your PA system or mixing board.

→ Getting used to hearing the live mix in a whole new way.

Custom In-Ear Monitors

Forget using off-the-shelf IEMs unless that's all your budget will allow for after also factoring in the cost of PMS hardware—you can always upgrade your IEMs to custom molds down the road. But keep in mind that the one-size-fits-all approach rarely works as well as the custom variety, even when the products include multiple-sized tips. If you want your IEMs to be comfortable and to provide the highest levels of sound isolation, you'll want them custom manufactured.

With custom molds, an audiologist makes an impression of your ear canals. The cost for this service tends to run in the $100–$200 range depending on where you live. Just like your fingerprints are unique, so are your ear canals. No two people's ear canals are identical, and in fact even your right and left ear canals can vary significantly from each other in their shape. That's why some earplugs can feel extremely uncomfortable, particularly ones that are made from plastic instead of foam. Fortunately, most of the off-the-shelf IEMs include foam tip options.

The process of getting your impressions made is pretty easy. After cleaning out your ear, the audiologist squirts some quick-drying foam or wax goo into your ears, and it conforms to the shape of your ear canals. The

Fig. 14.1: Custom graphics adorn these great-sounding IEMs from Ultimate Ears.

whole process takes five to ten minutes. If you're not sure where to find an audiologist who can make molds for you, most of the IEM manufacturers have searchable databases on their websites to assist you. A simple scan of your local Yellow Pages for audiologists or companies making/selling hearing aids will work, too.

Once you've got your molds/impressions made (people call them by both of these names interchangeably) and you've chosen a specific IEM model from one of a number of different manufacturers, you ship them your impressions and in just a couple of weeks, your personal IEMs are delivered.

Many companies make IEMs, and while the list of off-the-shelf products is exhaustive, the most popular custom IEM options come from Westone, Ultimate Ears, JH Audio, Sensaphonics, and Alien Ears. These companies offer many different models, and prices range from around $250 to $1,400.

If you have a set of off-the-shelf IEMs that you love the sound of, Alien Ears can manufacture custom molds that attach to your IEMs in place of the interchangeable tips, a nice solution that gets you a better fit and better sound isolation for less than $150 (IEMs not included, of course). They even supply a do-it-yourself impression kit—no trip to the audiologist necessary. Obviously, results may vary, but it's something worth checking out.

Just a few short years ago, IEMs typically had only one or two small drivers (speakers) in them, but recently, companies like those mentioned have pushed the envelope in small speaker design. The flagship JH Audio JH16 Pro packs eight drivers into each earpiece!

Why so many drivers in each IEM? To reduce distortion and deliver a clearer sound. With a passive crossover network in the IEM, different frequencies get directed to different drivers so that low frequencies don't mask high frequencies, mids cut through, and so on.

Obviously, the more drivers your IEMs incorporate, the more expensive they get. But even $300 custom IEMs are going to sound better than your favorite ear buds and, most importantly, provide the sound isolation benefit that protects your hearing. Other key features to look for in your custom molds: user serviceable cables! Use IEMs enough and you're bound to break the very thin audio cable connecting your IEMs to your bodypack. If the cable is hard-wired to the monitor, you'll have to send it back for servicing. But better models have detachable cables that can be replaced as simply as any other instrument cable.

Other options include ambient noise features to allow some of the room into your ears (more about this below), and one of our favorites: the ability to get custom colors and custom artwork placed on your IEMs! Sure, you could stick with a flesh colored IEM, but that's so . . . hearing aid! Encrust your IEM in Swarovski crystals, have a little alien or super hero, whatever you can think of.

Different IEMs from the various manufacturers are better suited to different types of musicians, too, with different ranges of frequency response. Some models are optimized for low end (bass players and drummers), some with a mid-range hump (guitarists), some with less low end (vocalists), and so on. So don't assume that your drummer's IEMs are the right model for you if you're a lead vocalist. Ultimate Ears even offers in-ear reference monitors for studio professionals searching for a flat frequency response similar to studio near-field monitors for use whether making mixes by laptop or recording live performances.

Custom IEMs provide incredible amounts of sound level reduction—routinely in the ballpark of -25 to -35 dB worth of sound isolation. Leave your noise-cancelling headphones home on your next airplane journey and just hook these up to your iPod or tablet. You'll be in heaven, from both the noise reduction and the incredible difference in audio quality over standard ear buds.

While you're getting a set of custom-fit IEMs, also consider getting some custom ear plugs! For much less than the cost of IEMs, custom earplugs can be manufactured from your impressions. Unlike those inexpensive foam plugs, these reduce volume without killing high-end frequencies and destroying the sound of music. And unlike those rubberized, ribbed earplugs, these fit like a glove. Comfort is king when it comes to actually putting hearing protection gear to regular use.

Personal Monitoring Systems (PMS)

Now that you've got your IEMs, it's time to begin monitoring your audio, and personal monitoring systems are made by all the leading wireless companies, including Shure, Sennheiser, Audio-Technica, and Lectrosonics.

If you've worked with wireless instrument systems before, the principles are the same (but backwards): you have a bodypack receiver that you wear and a transmitter that interfaces with your PA system or mixing board. Unlike your instrument systems, PMS products typically offer stereo operation, dual-mono (Shure calls this MixMode), and traditional mono output.

One of the decisions you'll have to make is whether you want to run full stereo or dual-mono. The bodypack typically offers an L/R balance control,

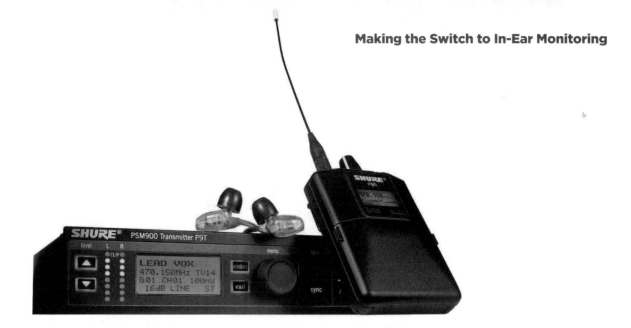

but its behavior varies depending on your monitoring configuration. In a traditional stereo setup, it functions just as you would imagine. In the dual-mono scenario, it typically acts as a balance level for two signals that are each delivered in mono. What this means is that the monitor mix being sent to each channel is heard in mono across both of your ears, and the balance control acts as a level control to make one of those signals louder or softer. Many musicians we know tend to favor running their IEM mixes in this mode, as you can have the music in one mix and vocals in the other, and the balance knob lets you raise or lower the vocals in your monitor mix. Or some players like to have their personal instrument in one mix and everything else in the other, or whatever other scenario you can think of.

If you've got good stereo monitoring options available from the mixing board, though, the stereo mix works great, as you can build a beautiful studio-like monitoring mix just for yourself. You can always have your sound guy make your vocals and your instrument louder than other people in the mix.

With most PMS devices, you can purchase additional receivers for multiple musicians to share the same monitor mix, but if everybody wants a custom mix, you'll need to purchase multiple systems. As a result, most touring bands have a rack filled with multiple PMS transmitters.

As you climb the price ladder with personal monitoring systems (they start under $300, with most of the pro stuff being in the $800–$1,200 range), you gain better audio specs, more wireless frequencies, more rugged construction, more detailed features, the ability to manage multiple wireless systems via computer software (essential for touring pros), greater broadcast distance, and so on.

The incredible Lectrosonics Quadra system gives you four channels of audio, personally mixable on your bodypack. With this solution, you could have a stereo mix of the band, one mono channel for your bass, and one channel for your voice, and you could adjust things as needed.

One thing that all PMS receivers have in common with each other—the most critical piece of the IEM solution—is brick-wall limiting. This circuitry prevents unwanted spikes in audio signals from reaching your ears. Unlike a loud pop or instrument blast coming through the PA or your floor wedges, when you've got IEMs inserted in your ears, completely isolating the sound, you could face serious hearing damage from an accidental volume spike.

Because of this significant risk, when monitoring audio via IEMs, unless you have personal and immediate control over the volume, or you know for a fact that a brick-wall limiter is installed in the signal path in the studio, never plug your IEMs directly into a headphone output on a mixer, instrument, or DI. All it takes is a millisecond to cause permanent damage or hearing loss.

Hooking Up Your PMS

Just because your band rents hourly rehearsal time doesn't mean you can't bring along your personal monitoring system. It's even becoming somewhat common for bands to bring their PMS gear with them to local club gigs. In both of these scenarios, all you need to do is install a couple of your transmitters in a small 2U or 4U rack and get a bunch of cables for connecting them to the mixing board. I'd suggest leaving the cables plugged into the back of this compact rack, attaching labels to the ends of the cables, and just coiling them up in the back of the rack when not in use.

If your mixer has a spare stereo output, you can easily run that output into a PMS transmitter for a stereo monitor mix, but most typically, you'll take advantage of the auxiliary outputs or bus outputs from your mixer.

An analog mixer like the popular Mackie SR-24 has six aux outputs and four subgroup outputs, while a digital mixer like the PreSonus StudioLive 24.4.2 has ten aux outputs and four subgroup outputs. Depending on the number of buses available to you, you'll be able to create more or less individual monitor mixes for the musicians in your band.

In the case of the StudioLive 24.4.2, for example, you could create five stereo IEM mixes or ten mono mixes, enough to give a large ensemble plenty of customized listening. Or you could use some of your sends for power amps and floor wedges—for those players in your band still doing it "old school," while your vocalists and drummer get in-ear mixes.

Connecting the personal monitoring system to your mixer isn't the end of your efforts, though. If you've purchased custom IEMs, you're going to find that almost all you can hear in your IEMs is . . . whatever is running through the mixing board! In most rehearsal scenarios, you probably don't have your drums, guitar amps, and bass amps miked. But if you want to hear these instruments in your monitor mix, you're going to have to throw up some mics. Of course, if you have a cabinet simulator like the fantastic Two Notes Torpedo Live, you won't need to mike your speaker cabinet at all.

No need to get extravagant with the drum kit, but for best results you should at least set up a pair of overheads and a kick drum mic, while a DI from the bass head and an SM-57 on your guitar amp should cover the rest . . . or a Two Notes Studio Live, of course!

If you have a stereo guitar rig and you're running the PMS in stereo, you'll obviously need a second mic, but get ready for the bliss of really hearing your stereo effects in the live scenario.

Adapting to the Sound of Silence

There are some key differences in the listening experience when you switch to IEMs. Obviously, it's going to sound as good or bad as you've mixed instruments and vocals, and generally, this is the beauty of in-ear monitoring. You get to bring the pristine studio sound to your live performances. And that's where things get messed up for some players! Some guitar players may find it unsettling not to really feel the presence of their rig behind them. Not to worry, though. Unless you've radically reduced your stage levels, you'll still feel the breeze from your 4×12 ruffling your pants, and tons of guitar players in rock and metal have made the switch from wedges.

The other thing missing by default is the sound of your audience! In a live venue, it's common to throw up a stereo mic to capture the ambience of the room and the crowd, and there's really no reason you can't throw up a room mic in your rehearsal space, too.

To further deal with the live "feel," some IEM manufacturers have incorporated optional ambient noise features. The simplest feature involves drilling tiny holes into the IEMs to allow ambient noise to enter your ears. The manufacturer usually provides a tiny rubber plug to blog the ambient port when it isn't needed, but really, bringing in the outside room like this defeats the hearing protection feature of your IEM. And expect to misplace those little rubber plugs.

IEMs like the DRM Earz DRM-XSP take matters to another level: they built a microphone into their custom IEMs with a tiny volume control similar to what you'd find on a hearing aid. This solution gives you the sound isolation benefit of IEMs combined with personal control over the ambience level.

The Sensaphonics 3D Active Ambient system goes one step further by incorporating ambience features into both their custom IEMs and associated features in the matched wireless PMS. Mics on the IEMs capture the sound around you, and a switch on the bodypack enables you to select instantly between two different modes of operation: Performance mode lets you dial in the amount of ambient sound, while flipping a switch to Full Ambient mode changes the behavior of the IEMs so that the onboard mics deliver audio at unity gain (natural volume) and the level of the IEM mix is reduced so that the priority is on hearing your band mates, crew, the audience, etc.

No matter which solution you pursue, give yourself some time to adjust! Most typical rock musicians tend to take a couple of weeks before they find themselves really at home with using IEMs. And some players employ a hybrid approach that combines floor wedges and IEMs, allowing for natural ambience.

There are numerous ways to mix and match a solution that's right for your performance needs. But once you start using them, it can be very hard living without them. So the only real question is . . . when are you going to take the plunge?

Reprinted courtesy of MusicPlayers.com

Glossary

Effects Loop: A guitar amp or preamp section that enables interfacing with effects before the guitar signal reaches the power amp section.

Four-Cable Method: A way of connecting certain multi-effects processors with internal preamp loops where some effects are routed to the front of the amp and other effects are routed to the amp's effects loop. Stereo operation requires five cables.

Guitar Rig: The complete collection of gear used in delivering your sound, including amp(s), speaker cabinets, effects pedals, rack gear, foot controllers, etc.

Kill Dry: A feature of some effects processors that disables the internal mixer circuit so that only a wet (processed) signal is output. This is essential for use in a parallel effects loop.

Latency: The very short delay (usually measured in milliseconds) in a digital signal caused by passing through one or more pieces of digital audio equipment whose processing of that signal (even leaving it "unprocessed") results in delayed playback. Latency can make a performance sound out of sync with other audio signals (such as a guitar signal being recorded into a DAW sounding slightly delayed in your headphone mix). Tiny amounts of latency are normal and are typically unnoticeable.

Parallel Effects Loop: When a guitar signal is split so that part of it is routed directly to the amp's power amp section and part is sent via the Effects Send jack to the effects. A mix control allows control over the wet/dry balance of the send. The effected sound returns to the amp via the Effects Return jack(s), just before the power amp section.

Patch, Preset, or Program: A stored setting in an effects processor or a programmable amplifier. One patch may call up a particular digital delay plus reverb while another patch/program/preset may have a compressor, flanger, and wah. In your modeling device, one patch may load a Vox amp with reverb while another loads a Marshall amp with a Variac applied (virtually) to the output. Factory presets are the various combinations of sounds/settings that a manufacturer has preprogrammed into a device to show off its features and/or help you get started with your own sound design.

Phantom Power: Power supplied remotely to a MIDI foot controller over a MIDI cable. Typically uses DIN-7 MIDI cables.

Rack Gear: A broad category of products including amps, effects processors, power conditioners, and wireless systems that is configured to fit into a standard 19-inch-wide equipment rack.

Re-amping: A studio technique where an instrument's signal is recorded dry (sans amp) so that it can be sent back to one or more amps afterward to experiment with different tones. Alternatively, the dry signal can be run through amp-modeling hardware or plug-ins.

Series Effects Loop: Also called a serial loop. Where 100 percent of the guitar signal passes through the Effects Send to your effects pedals and/or rack gear, then returns to the amp through the Effects Return jack(s).

True Bypass: A capability of many effects products in which the signal passes directly through from input to output without going through any buffers or other audio circuits when the effects unit is disengaged/off.

Variac: Variable AC. A device that is sometimes used to reduce the amount of AC power running into an amplifier. Vintage Marshall amps were designed for 110V, but US current runs at 120V. With a Variac, you can reduce the incoming voltage to 110V to put less strain on the amp, or you could create a "brown" sound by reducing the incoming voltage to lower than what the amp needs. Just like running some pedals with half-drained batteries or reduced AC current, it may create a tonal variation that you like.

For Additional Information

Following is a list of all the manufacturers whose products are featured in this book. Be sure to visit their websites to discover the full range of products available. This book only featured select items in a much larger collection of rig-building tools.

Also, be sure to visit www.musicplayers.com/mgr for supplemental materials related to the book, such as product pricing, additional rig building information, and more.

Audio-Technica
www.audio-technica.com

Axess Electronics
www.axess-electronics.com

BOSS
www.bossus.com

Calzone Case Co.
www.calzonecase.com

Carl Martin
www.carlmartin.com

Cusack Effects
www.cusackeffects.com

Custom Audio Electronics
www.customaudioelectronics.com

DigiTech
www.digitech.com

Dunlop
www.jimdunlop.com

Guitar Laboratory
www.glab.com.pl

Egnater Amplification

www.egnateramps.com

Electro-Harmonix

www.ehx.com

ENGL Amplifier

www.engl-amps.com

Eventide

www.eventide.com

Fishman Transducers

www.fishman.com

Fractal Audio Systems

www.fractalaudio.com

Fryette Amplification

www.sfdamp.com

Furman

www.furmansound.com

Gator Cases

www.gatorcases.com

George L's

www.georgels.com

Graphtech Guitar Labs

www.graphtech.com

Highlite International

www.highlite.nl

ISP Technologies

www.isptechnologies.com

Korg

www.korg.com

Lava Cable
www.lavacable.com

Lectrosonics
www.lectrosonics.com

Lehle
www.lehle.com

Line 6
www.line6.com

L.R. Baggs
www.lrbaggs.com

Mark L Custom Guitar Electronics
www.marklcustom.com

Matrix Amplification
uk.matrixamplification.com

Maxline Music Cases
www.maxlinemusiccases.com

Middle Atlantic Products
www.middleatlantic.com

Mesa/Boogie
www.mesaboogie.com

Monster Power
www.monstercable.com

Musicom Lab
www.musicomlab.co.kr

One Control
www.one-control.com

Palmer
www.palmer-germany.com

Pete Cornish

www.petecornish.co.uk

Peterson Strobe Tuners

www.petersontuners.com

Planet Waves

www.planet-waves.com

Rackman

www.rackman.com

Radial Engineering

www.radialeng.com

Raxxess Metalsmiths

www.raxxess.com

Rhodes Amplification

www.rhodesamplification.com

Rivera

www.rivera.com

RJM Music Technology

www.rjmmusic.com

Robert Keeley Electronics

www.robertkeeley.com

Rock Hard Cases

www.rockhardcases.com

Rocktron

www.rocktron.com

Samson

www.samsontech.com

Sennheiser

www.sennheiser.com

SKB
www.skbcases.com

Skrydstrup R&D
www.skrydstrup.com

Sound Sculpture
www.soundsculpture.com

TC Electronic
www.tcelectronic.com

THD Electronics
www.thdelectronics.com

TheGigRig
www.thegigrig.com

Two Notes Audio Engineering
www.two-notes.com

VIsual Sound
www.visualsound.net

Voodoo Lab
www.voodoolab.com

Whirlwind
www.whirlwindusa.com

music PRO guides

Quality Instruction, Professional Results

Prices, contents, and availability subject to change without notice.

Hal Leonard Books
An Imprint of Hal Leonard Corporation
www.musicproguides.com

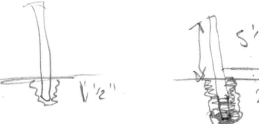

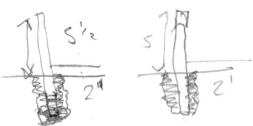

1'½"

5'½

2"

5

2'